Dream Big, Draw Bigger

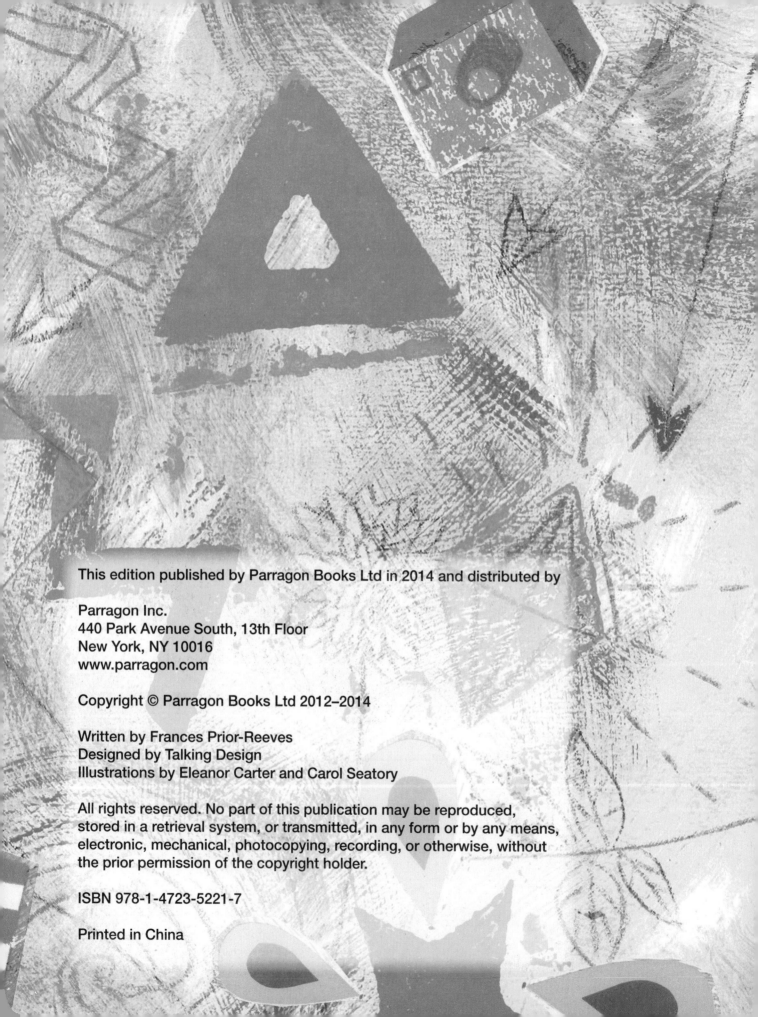

This edition published by Parragon Books Ltd in 2014 and distributed by

Parragon Inc.
440 Park Avenue South, 13th Floor
New York, NY 10016
www.parragon.com

Copyright © Parragon Books Ltd 2012–2014

Written by Frances Prior-Reeves
Designed by Talking Design
Illustrations by Eleanor Carter and Carol Seatory

ISBN 978-1-4723-5221-7

Printed in China

Dream Big, Draw Bigger

PaRragon

Bath · New York · Cologne · Melbourne · Delhi
Hong Kong · Shenzhen · Singapore · Amsterdam

"IN ART, AS THE BEST WAY REMEDY IS TO ADVANTAGE

IN *life,*
TO
mistakes
TAKE
OF THEM. "

Walter Darby Bannard.

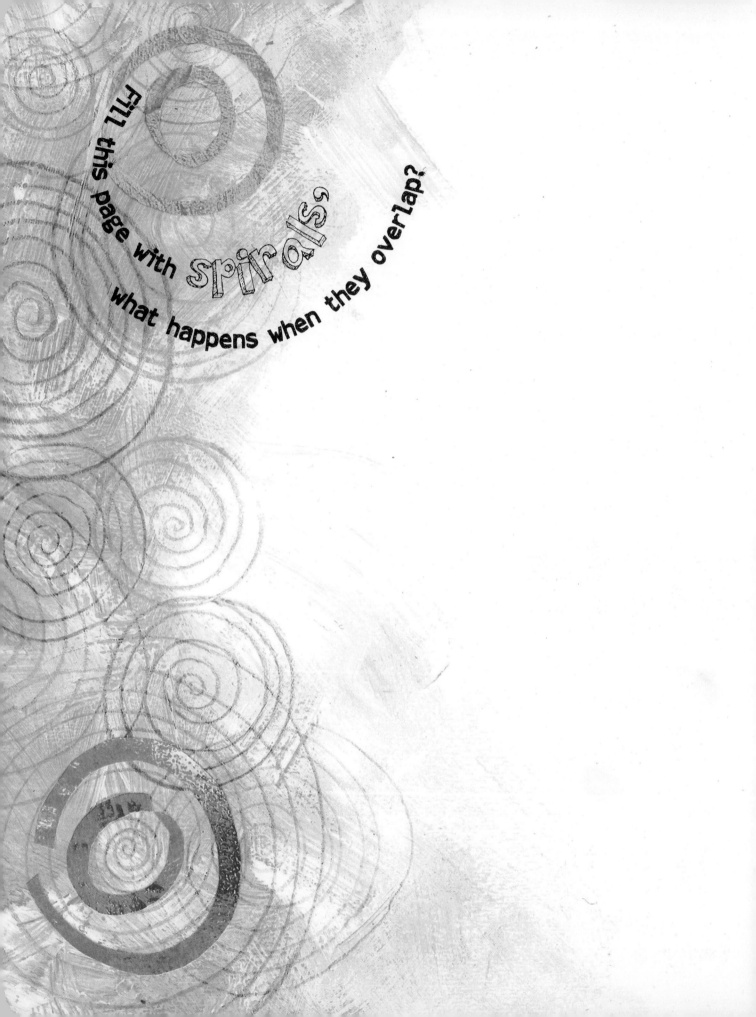

Fill this page with **spirals**, what happens when they overlap?

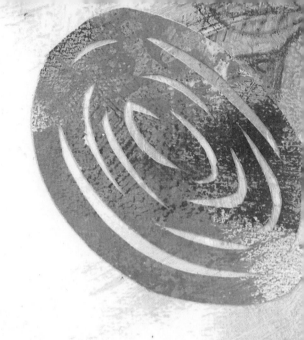

Can you create a whirlpool of color?

Fill this window box with
flowers.

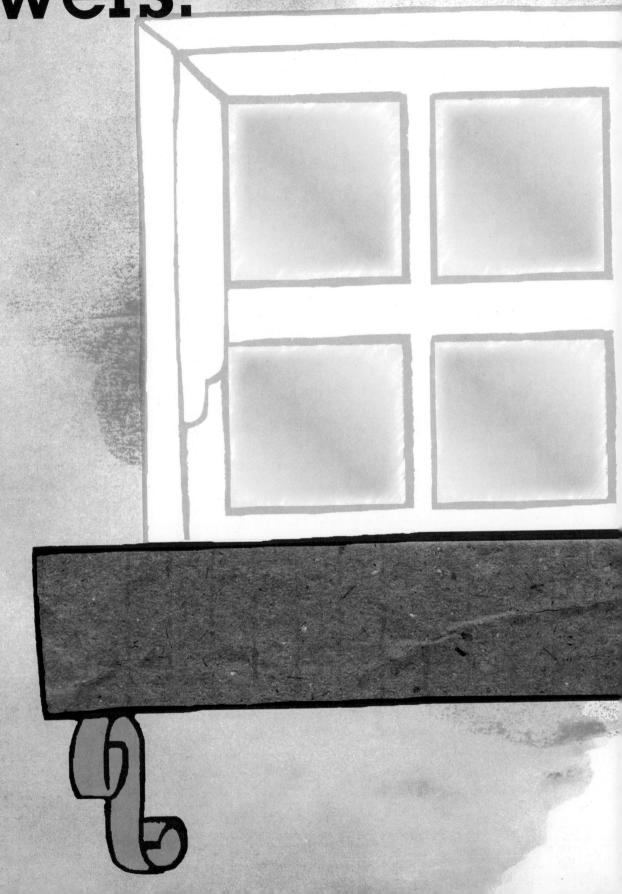

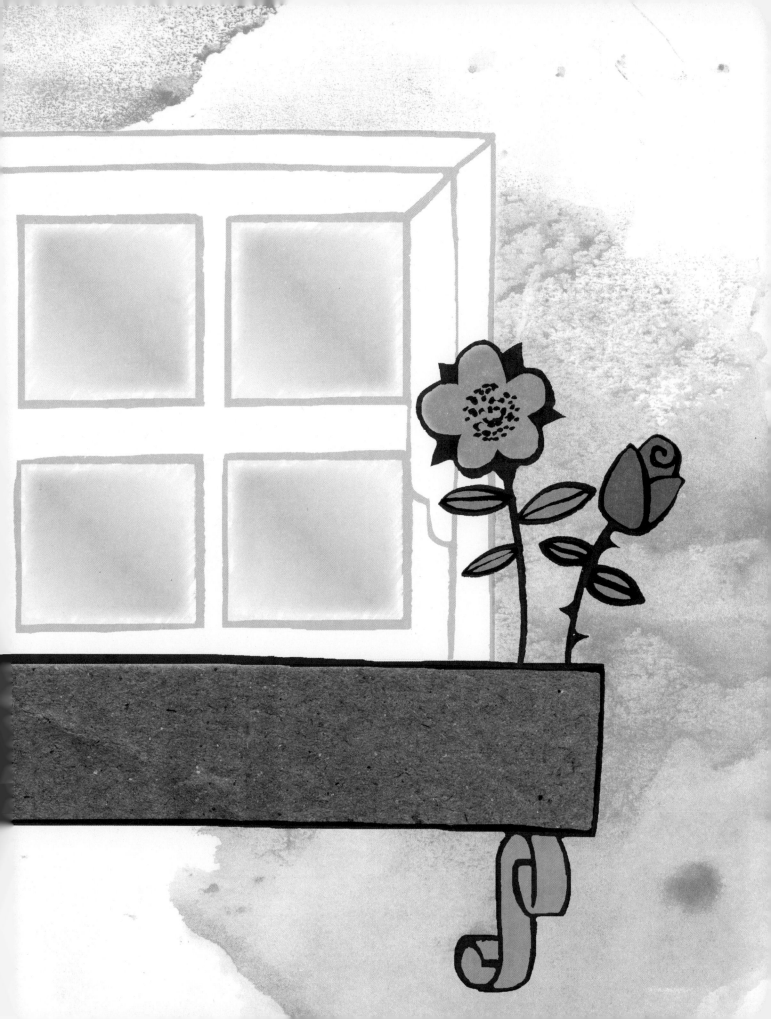

Draw this *bird's song.*

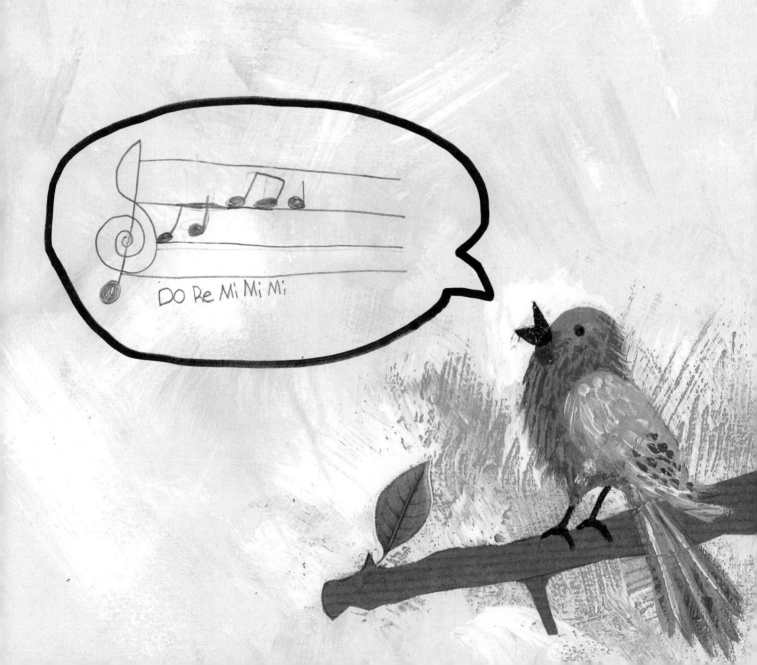

Fill this page with
cubes.

**Can you build an object
from those cubes?**

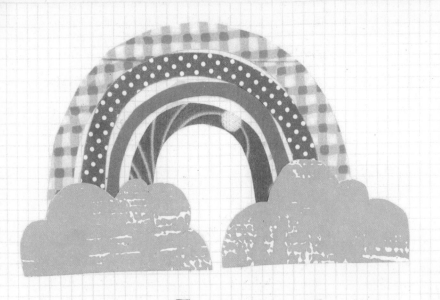

Draw your **happiest** mood.

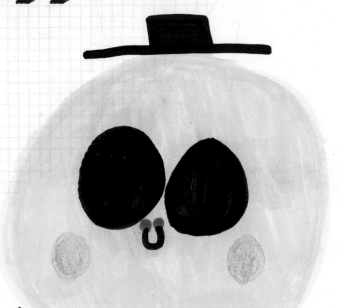

Always smile!

Draw your **SADDEST** mood.

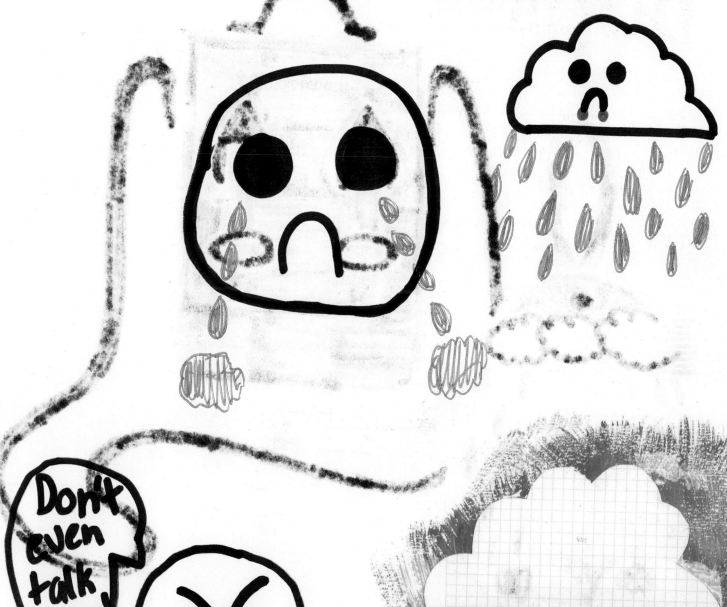

Draw your angriest mood.

Design these
bags.

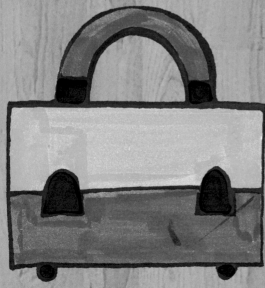
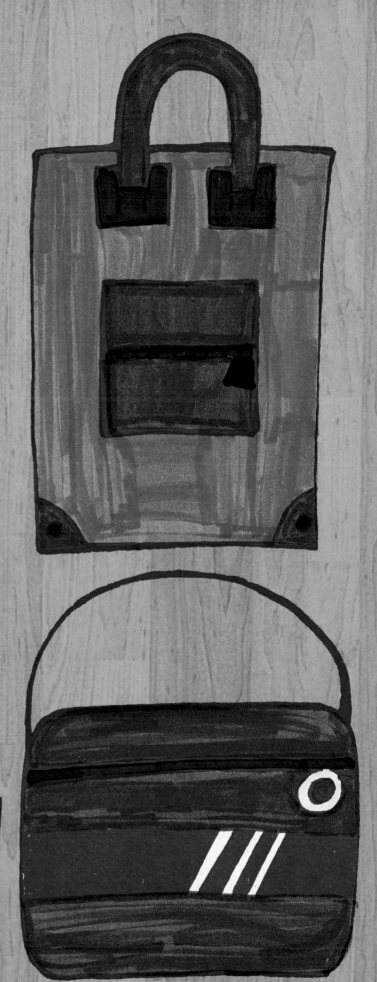
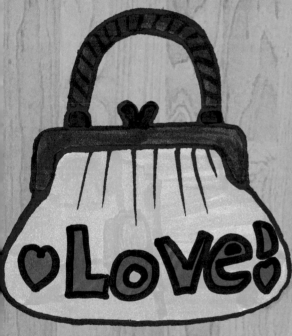

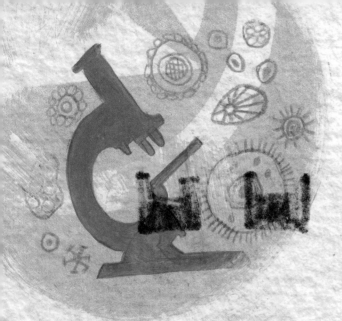

Draw something tiny.

Draw something
GIGANTIC.

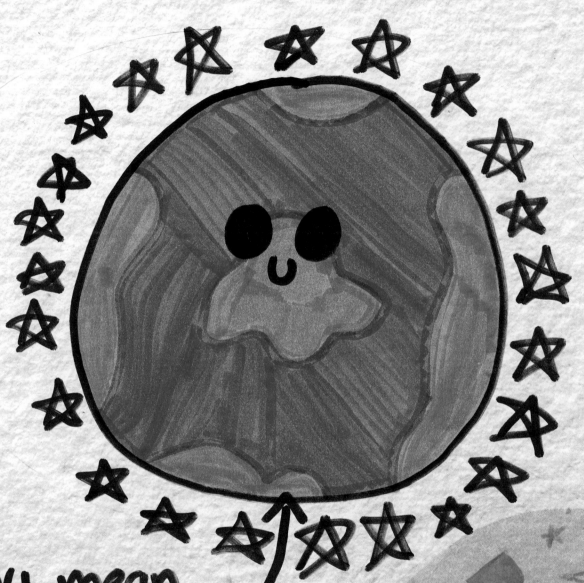

You mean the world to me.

Fill this jar

with candy canes.

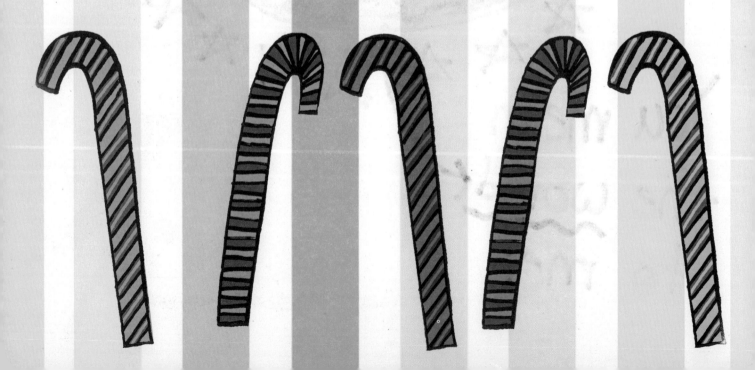

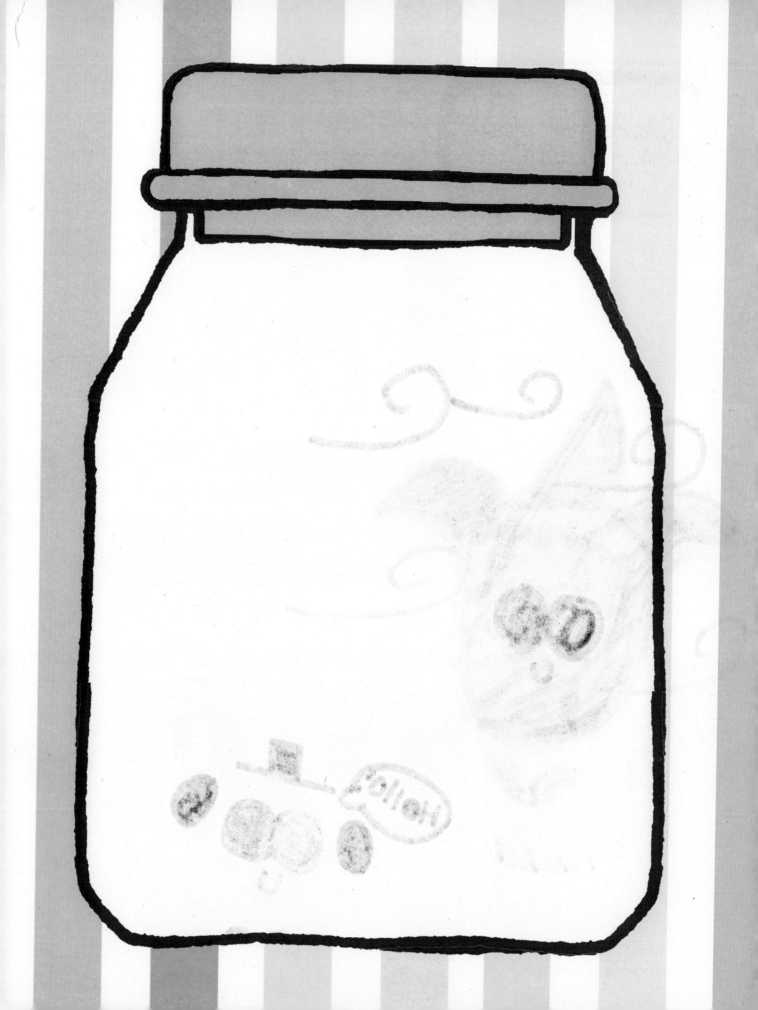

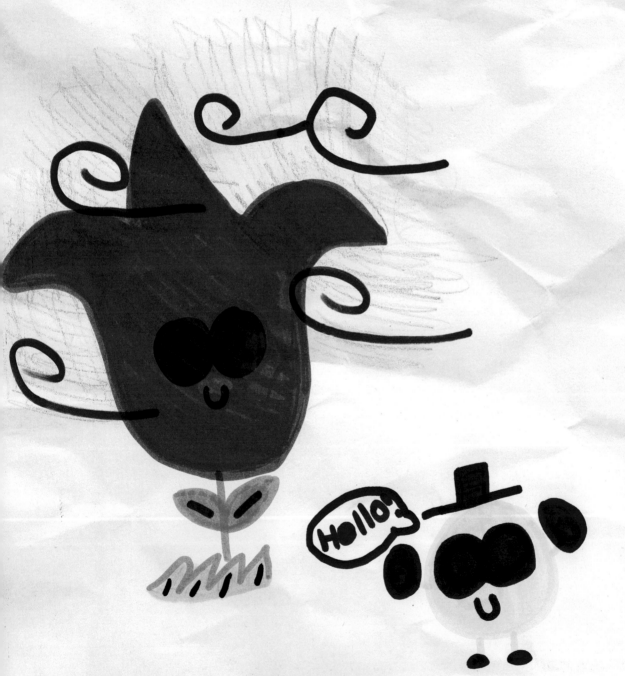

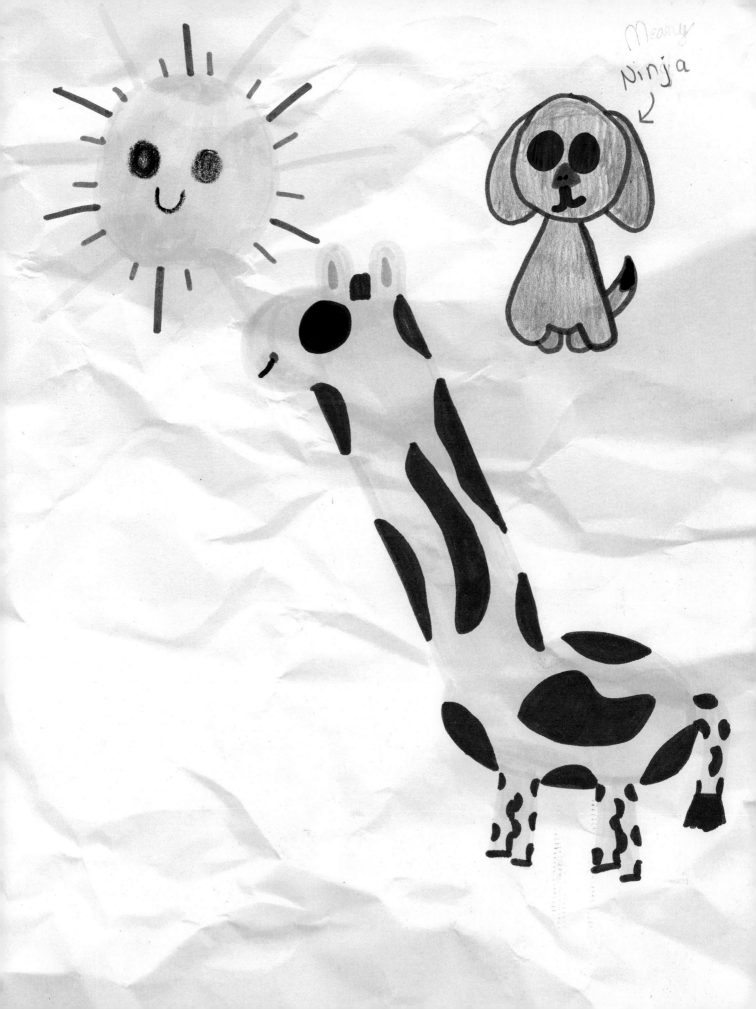

Draw your

IDEA.

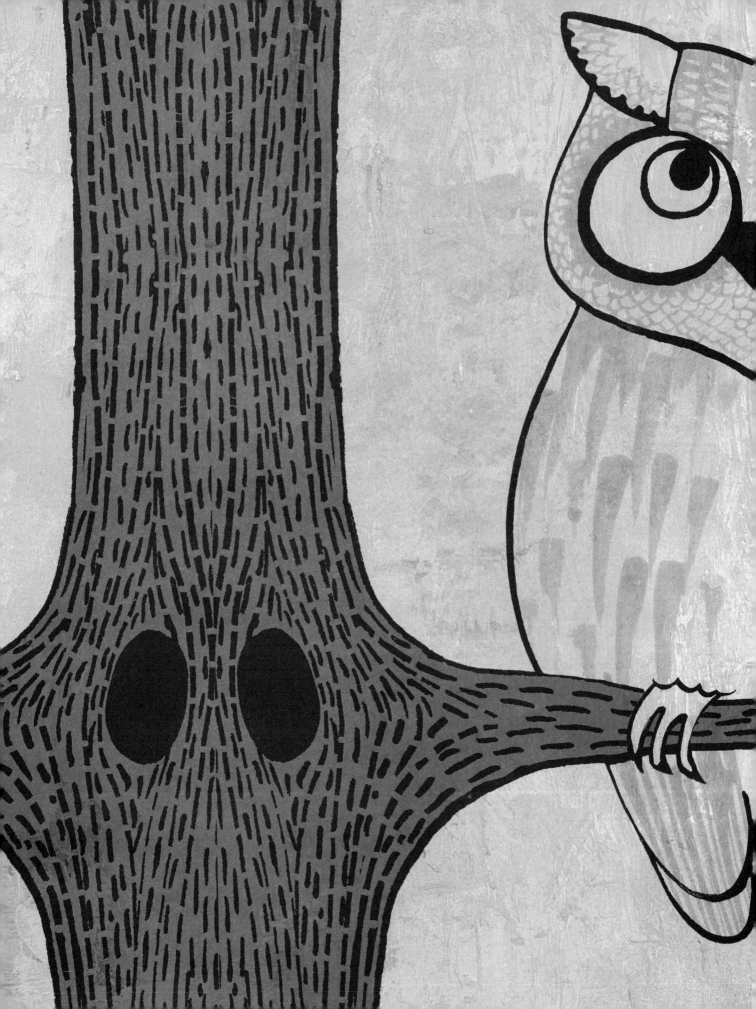

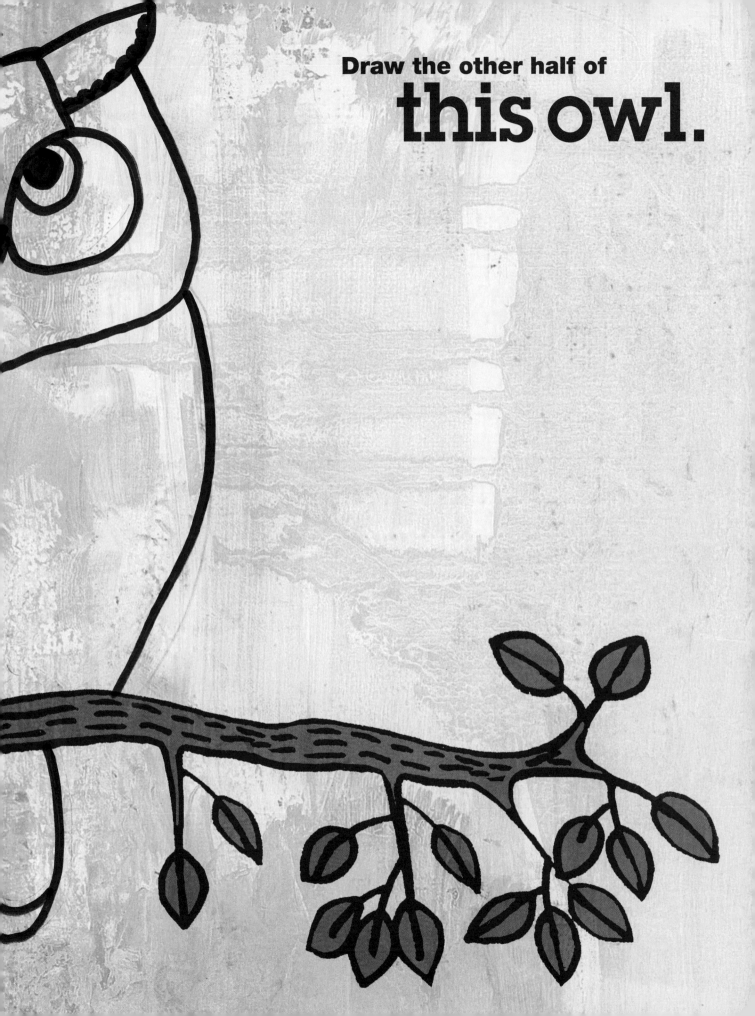

Draw the other half of
this owl.

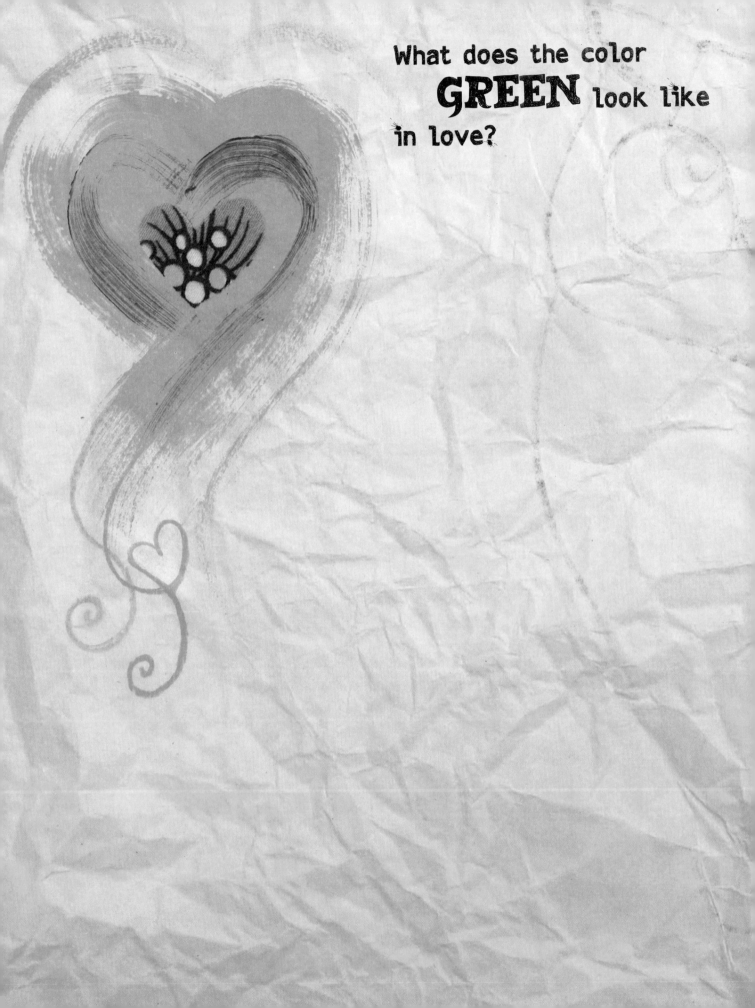

What does the color
GREEN look like
in love?

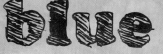

What does the color **blue** look like sunbathing?

Draw...

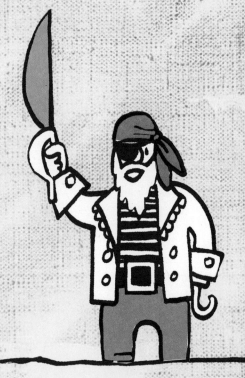

_a **pirate,**

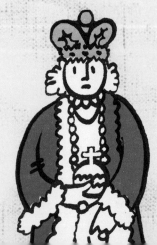

_a **queen,**

and a
magician.

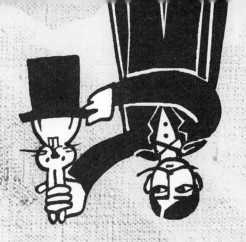

Now draw **one**
image of all three.

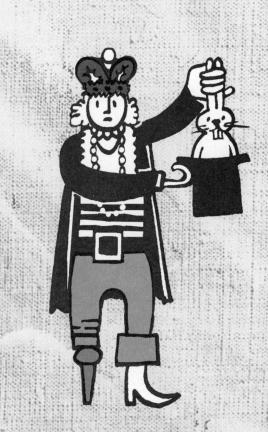

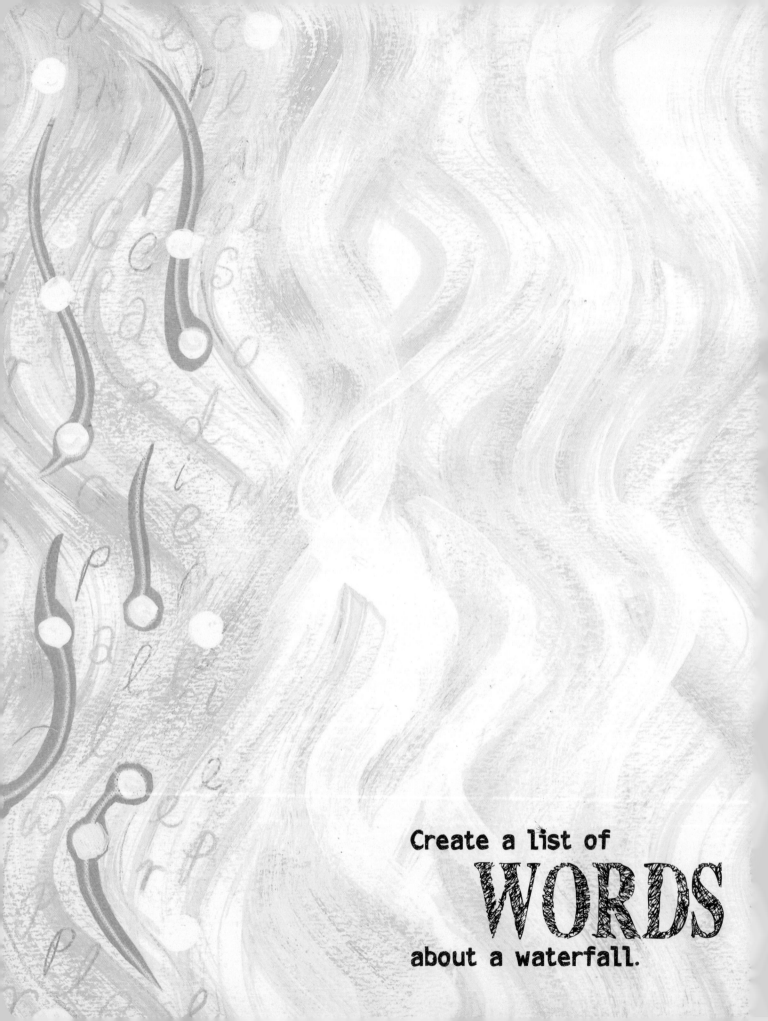

Create a list of
WORDS
about a waterfall.

Flow those words into an IMAGE.

Wrap this gift.

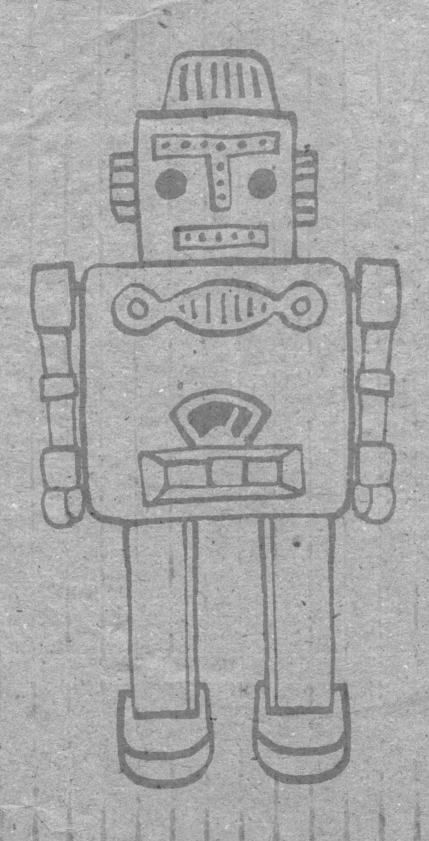

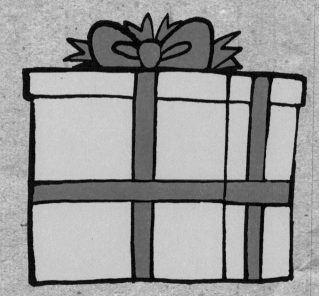

Unwrap

this gift in the space above, what is it?

Draw your favorite **song.**

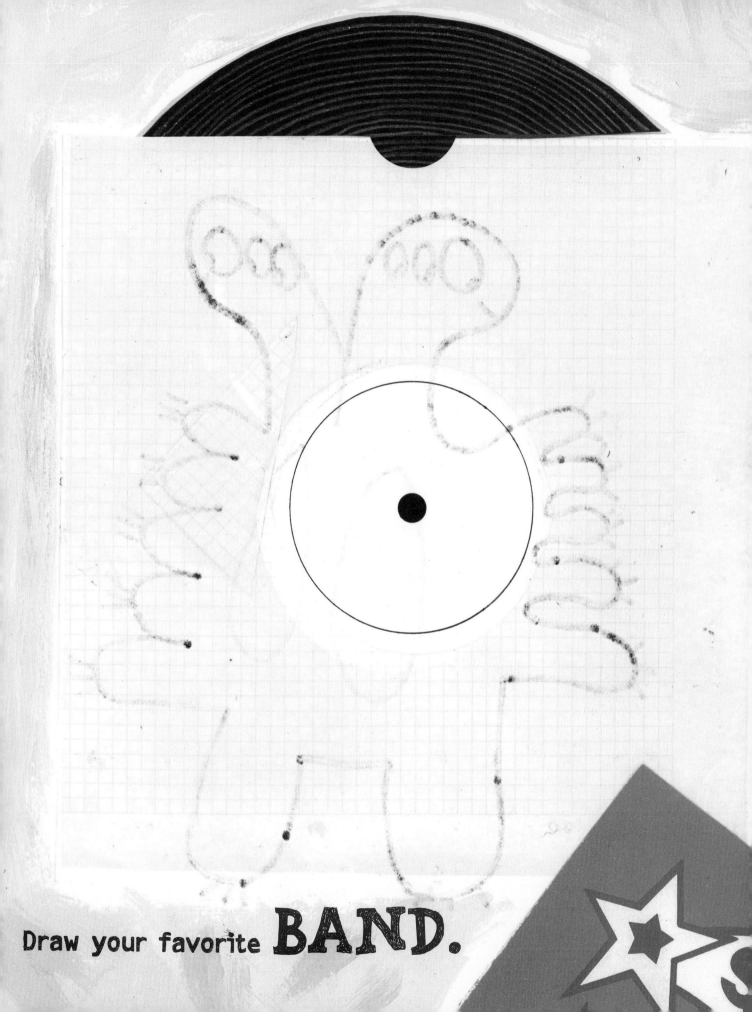

Draw your favorite **BAND.**

Draw a **monster**
with two heads, three eyes,
five arms, and one mouth.

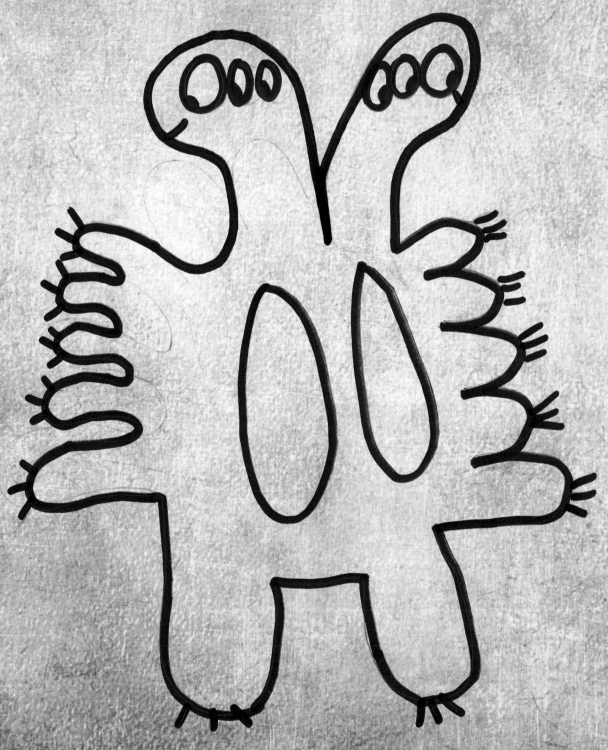

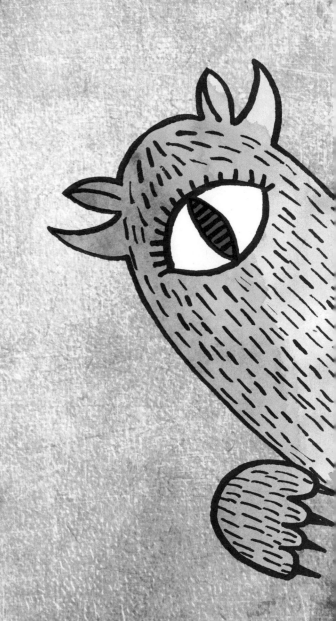

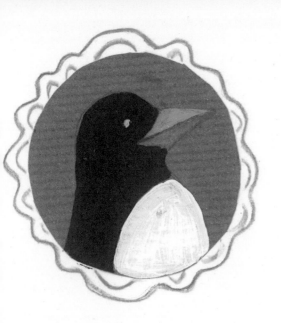

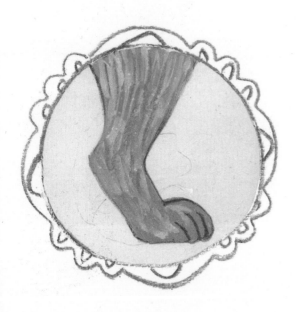

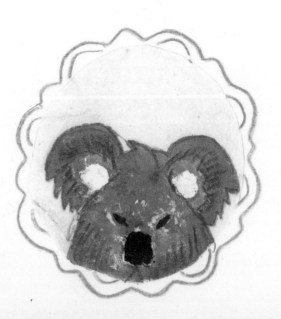

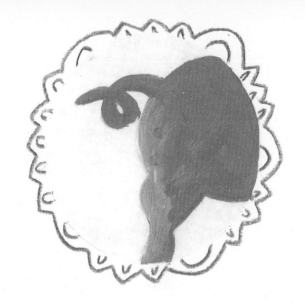

Draw an **animal** that combines your *five favorite* animals.

Draw the

autumn leaves

falling from this tree.

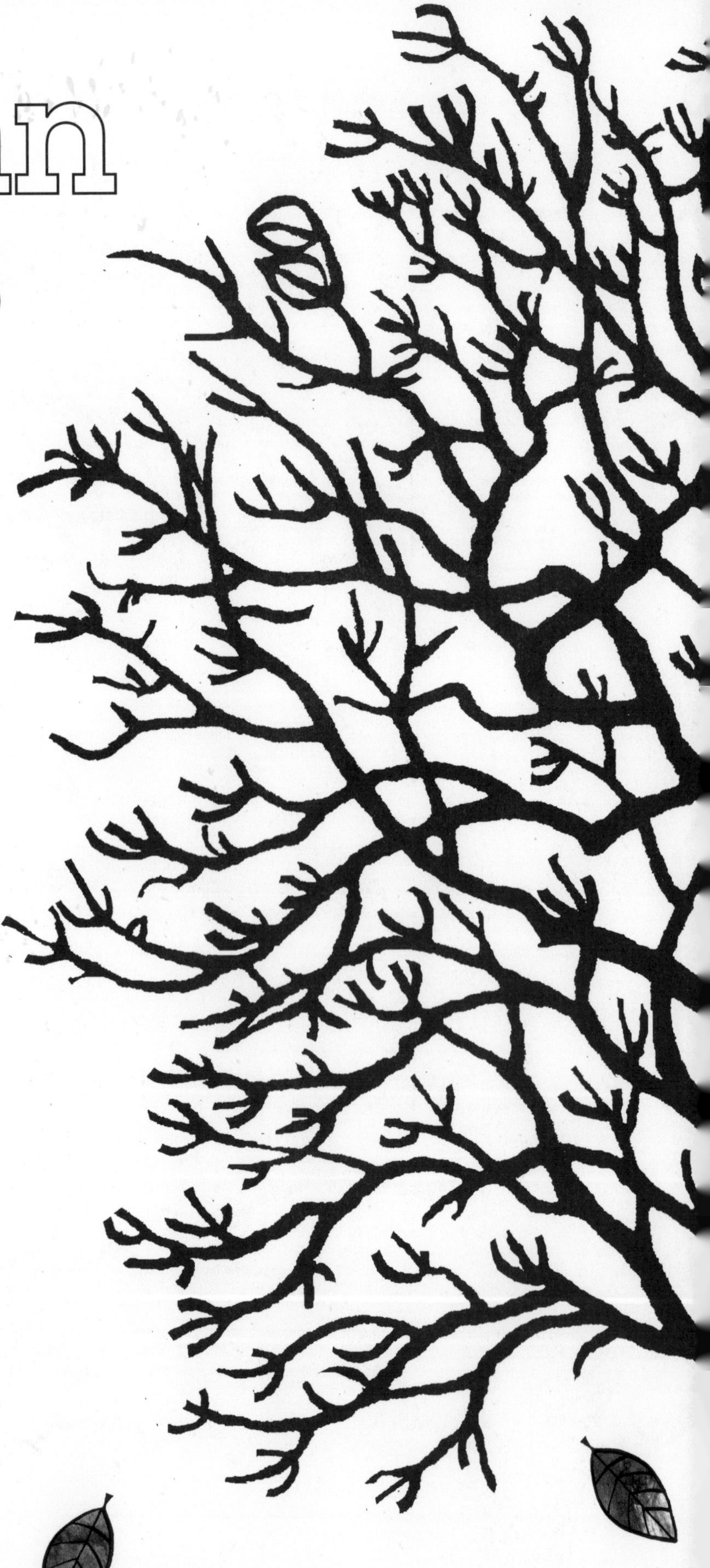

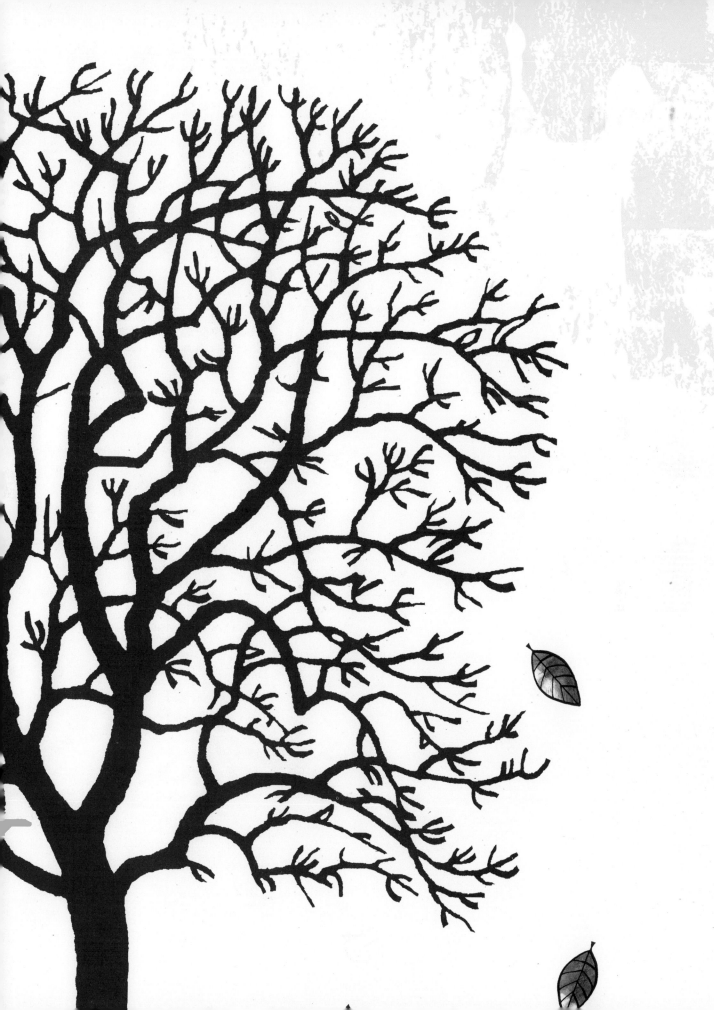

Doodles!
don't have to
be mindless.

Add some colorful
rain boots
splashing in these puddles.

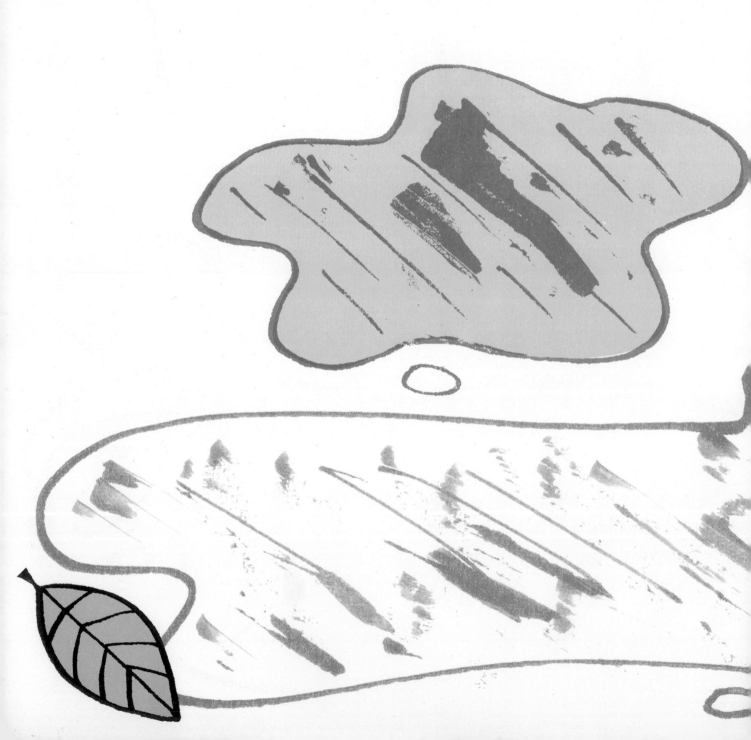

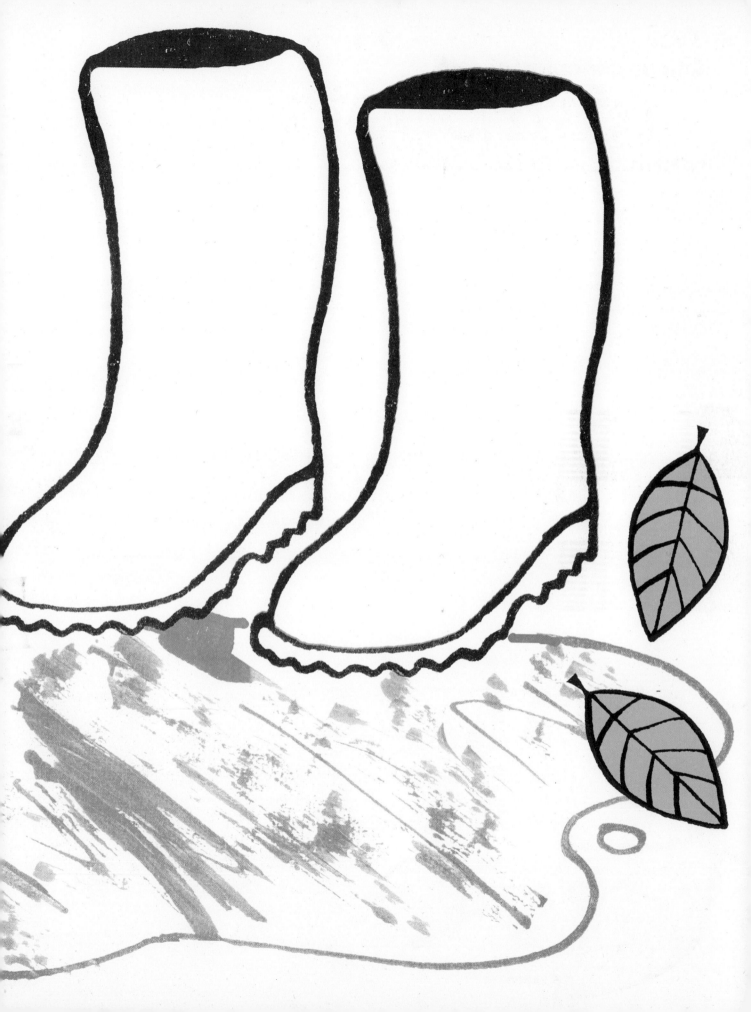

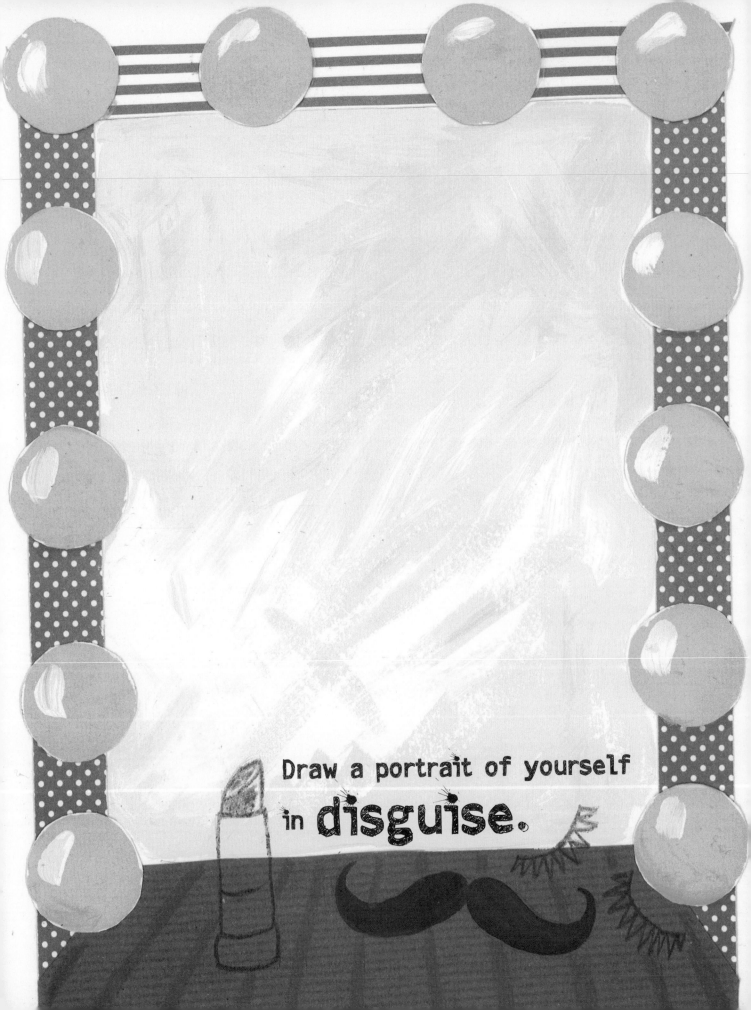

Draw a portrait of yourself in **disguise.**

Draw a portrait of **yourself**
with your *eyes closed.*

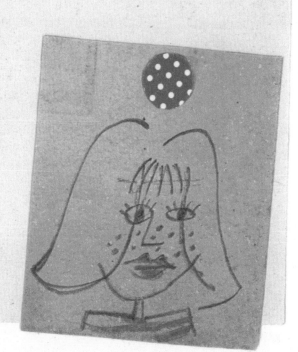

Draw the thing that goes

BUMP in the night.

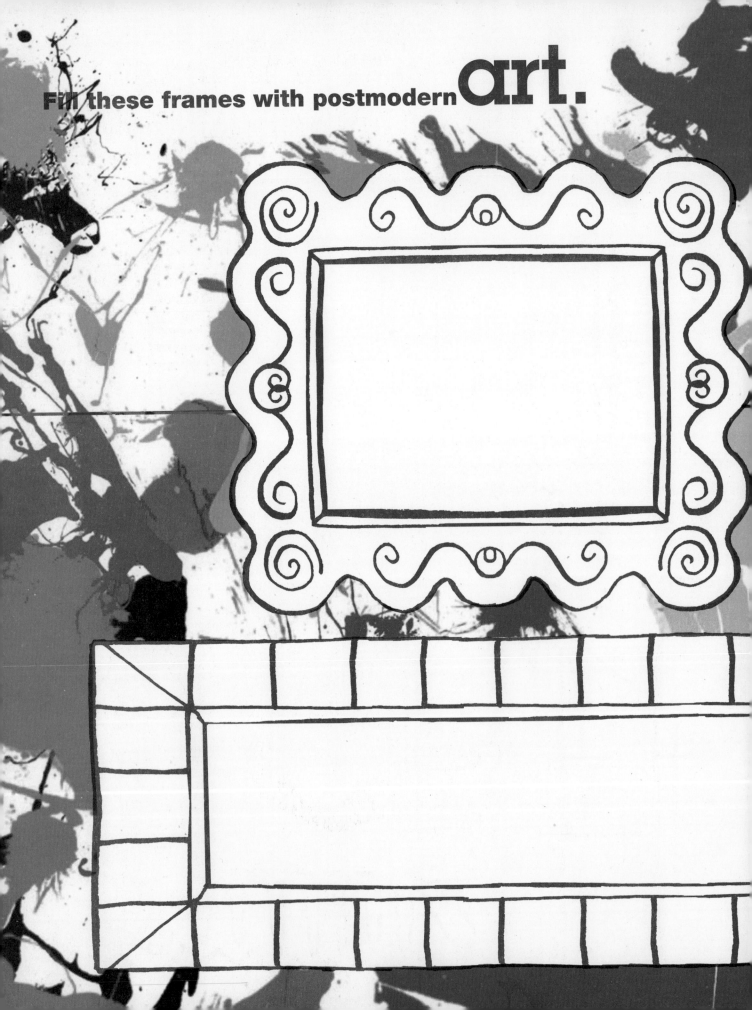

Fill these frames with postmodern **art.**

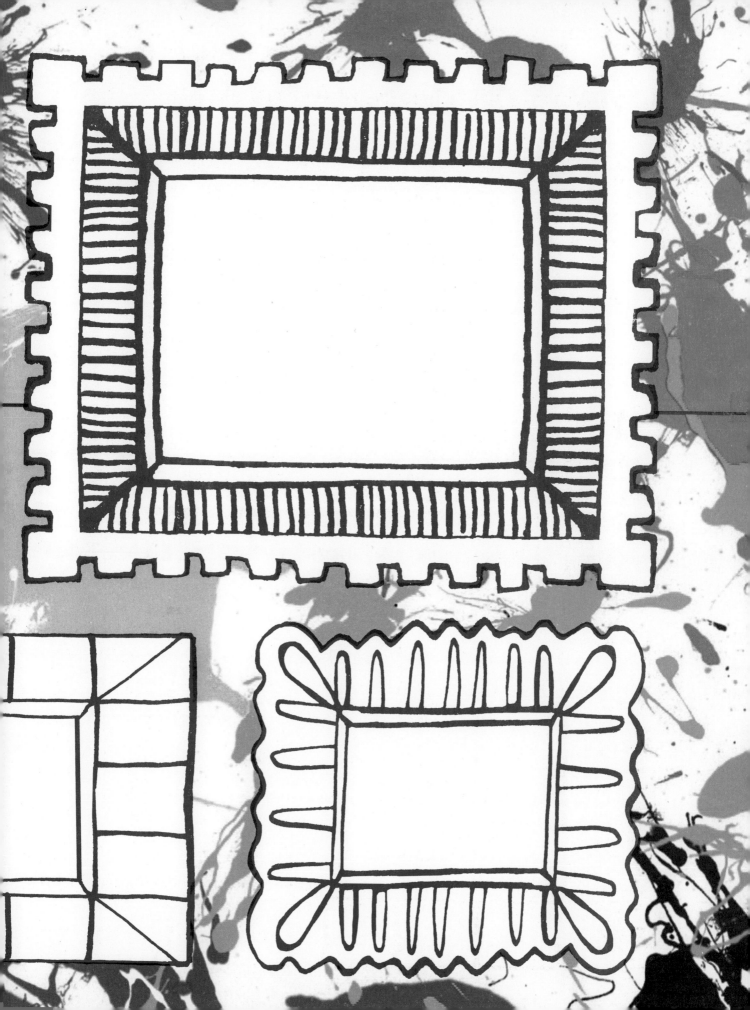

Draw a **Jealous** color.

Draw a **calm** color.

Draw **PURPLE**
and **yellow** in love.

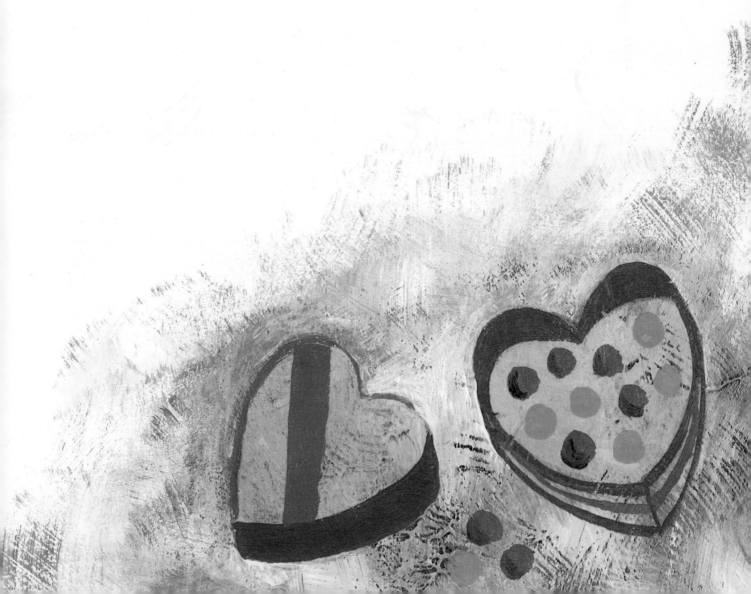

Draw an
octopus
having a fight with a
spider.

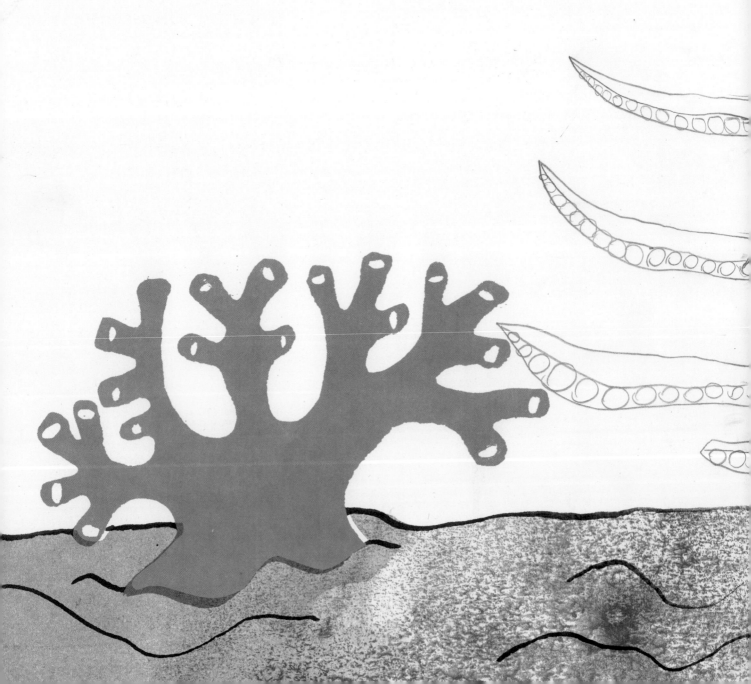

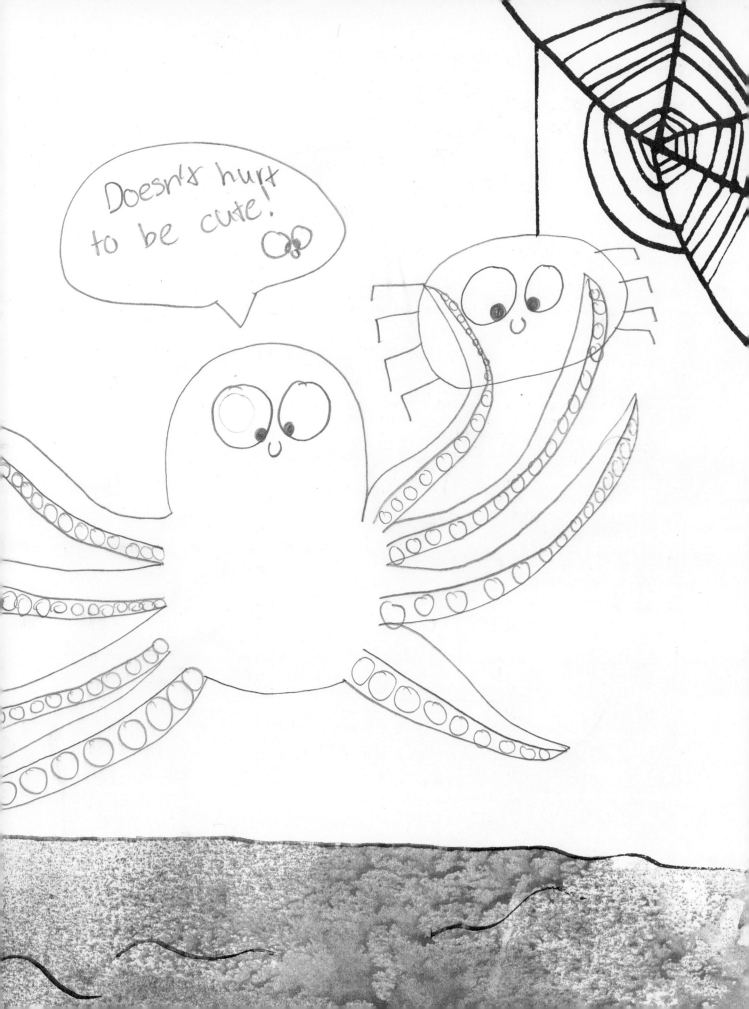

Draw once upon a **time.**

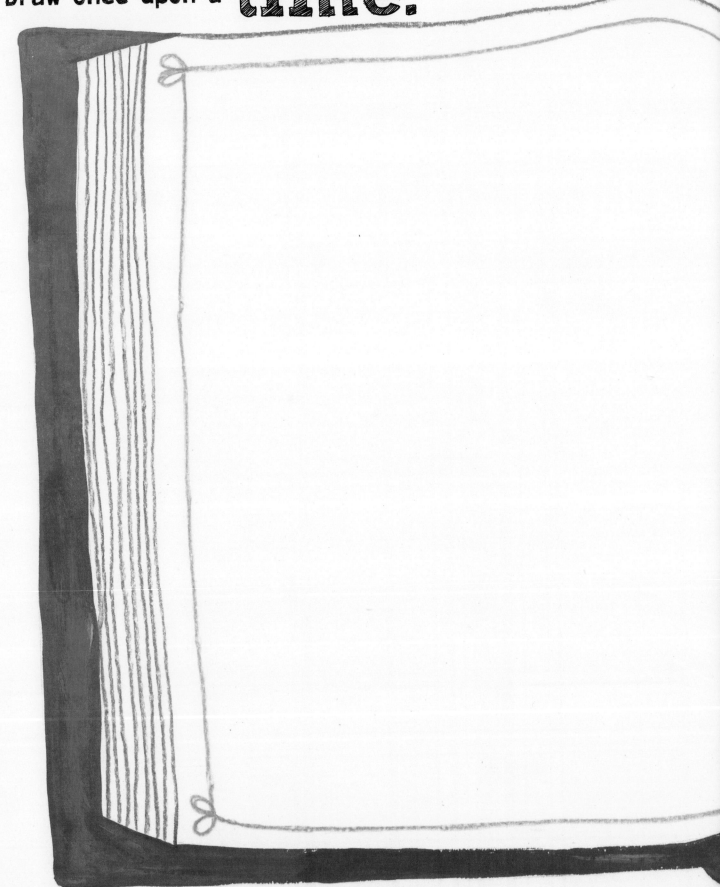

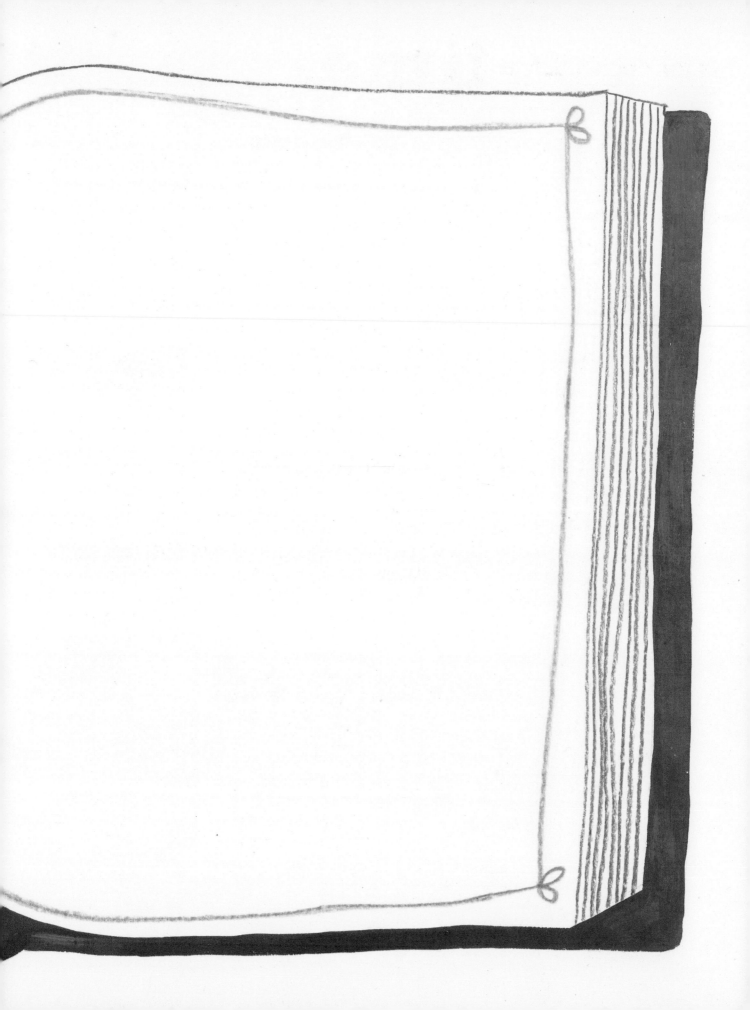

Draw **sandcastles**
on this beach.

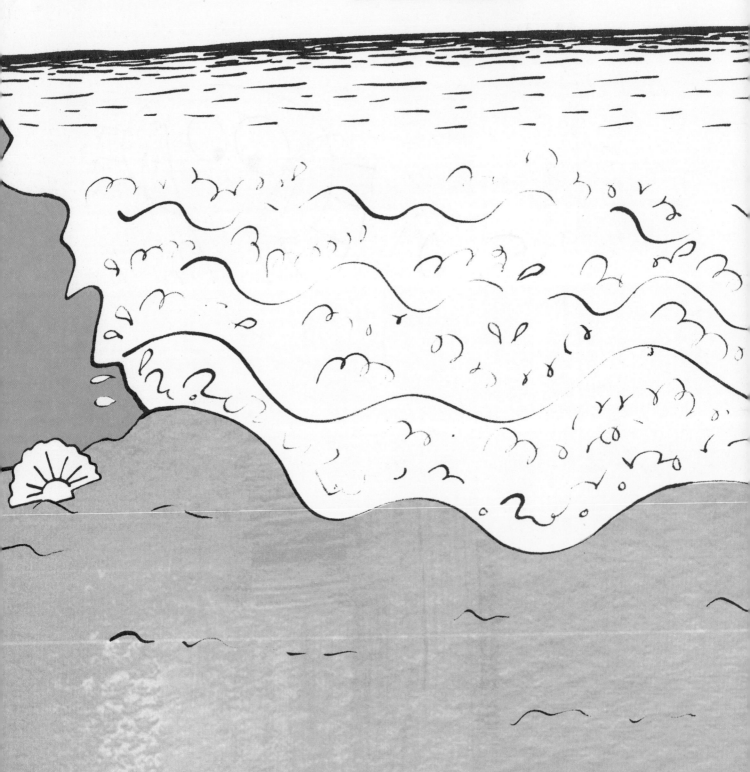

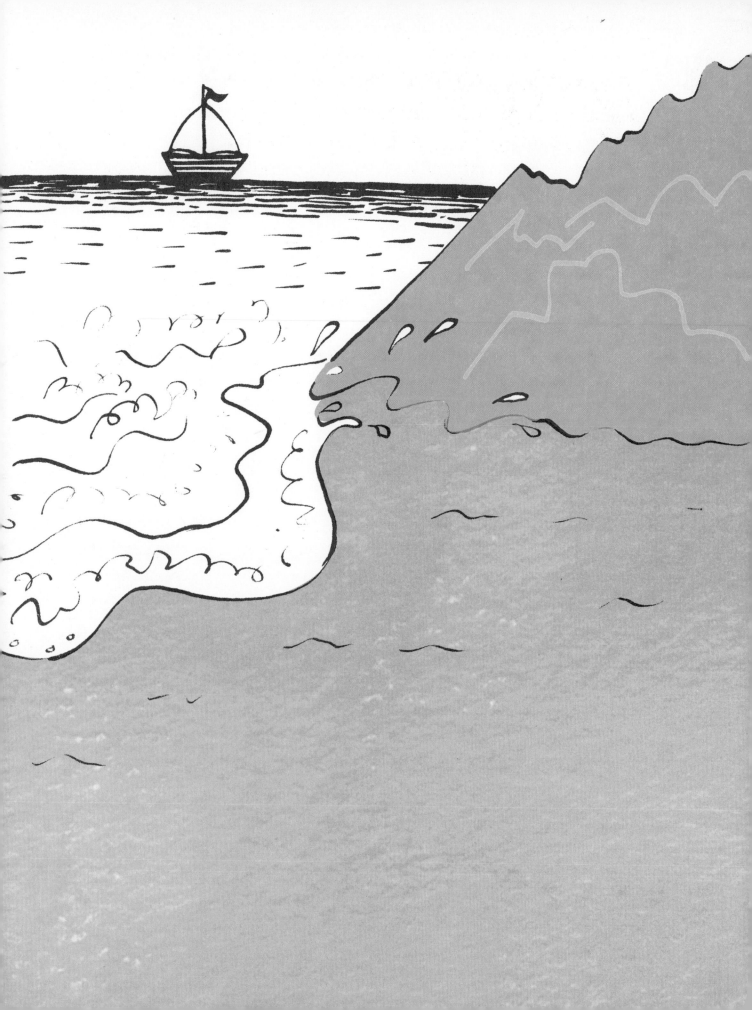

Draw a *mirage.*

Fill this page with
triangles.

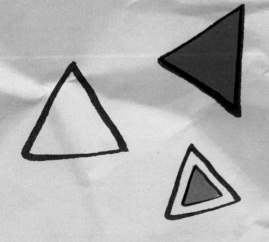

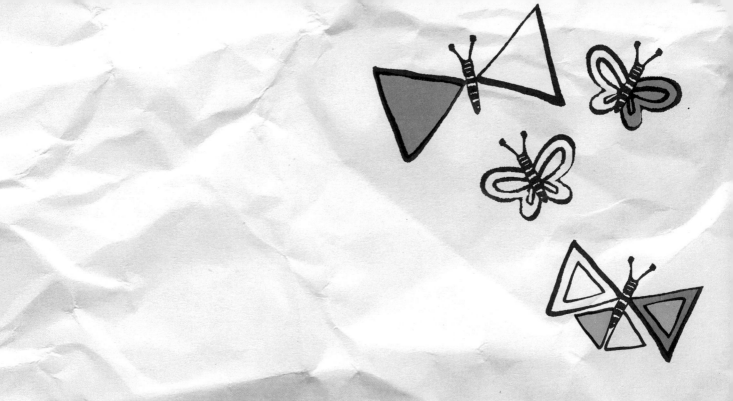

Can you turn those triangles into
butterflies?

"I found I could say things with color and shapes that I couldn't say any other way— things I had no words for."

Georgia O'Keeffe.

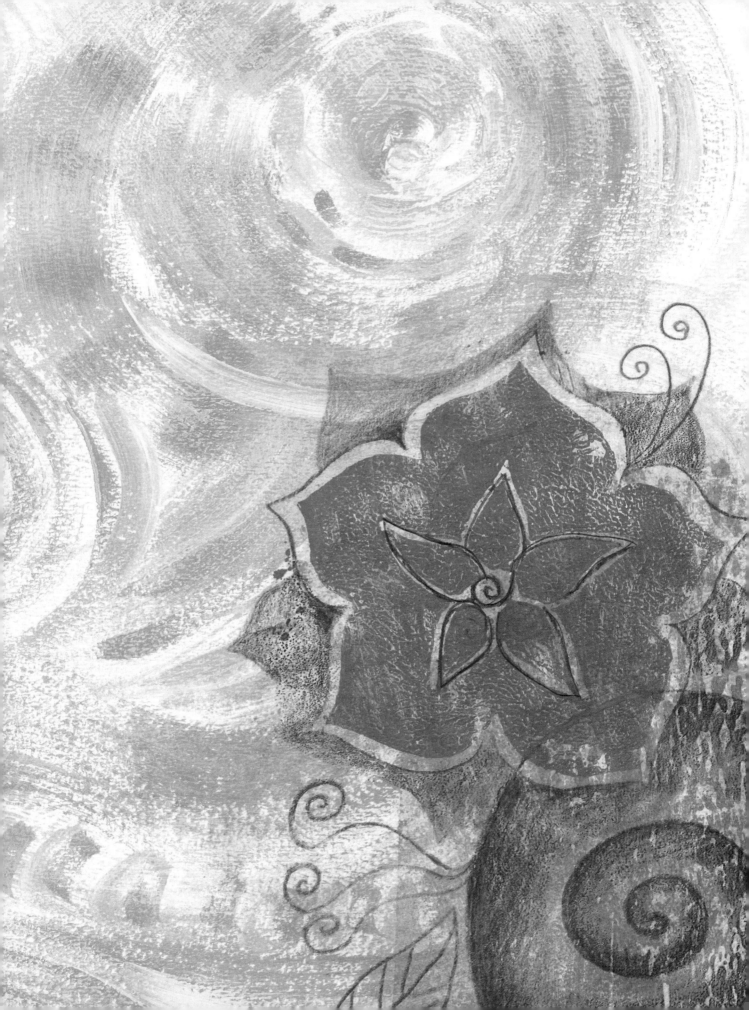

Fill this grassland with *life.*

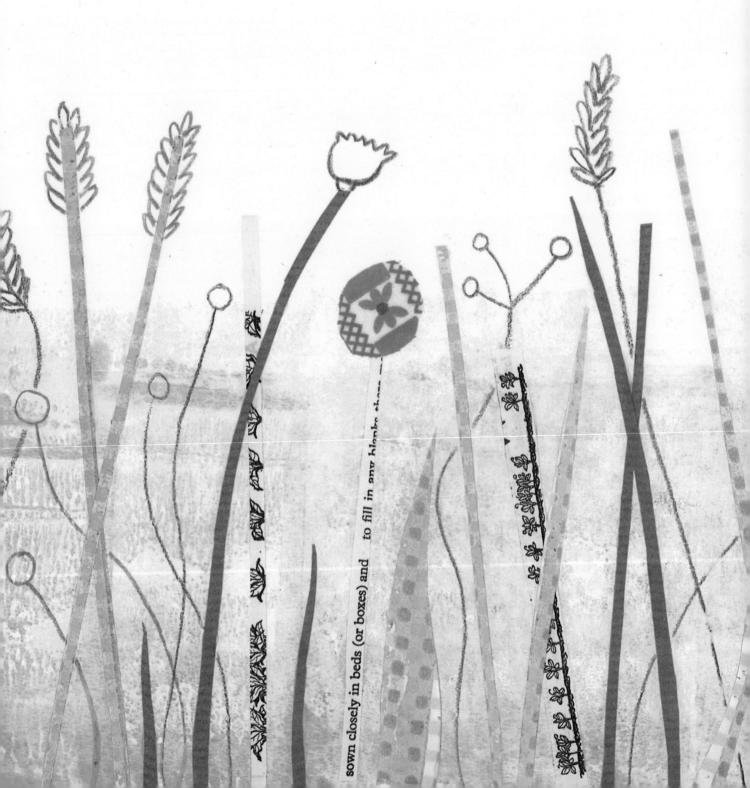

sown closely in beds (or boxes) and   to fill in any blank space

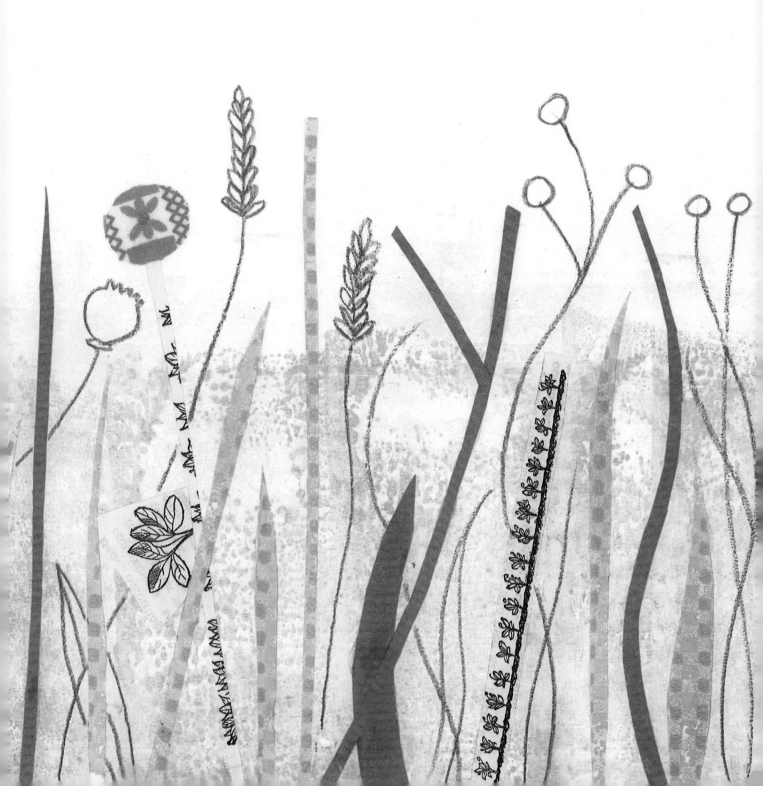

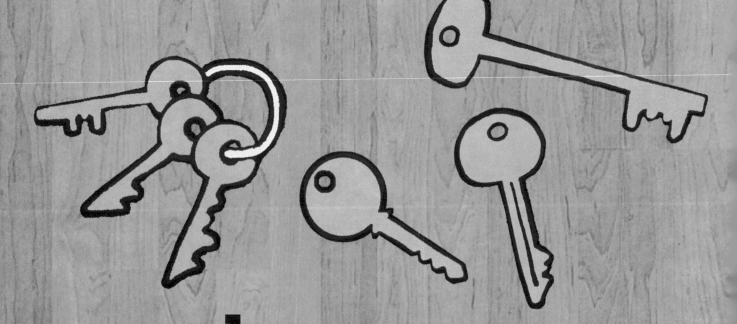

Fill this jar with keys.

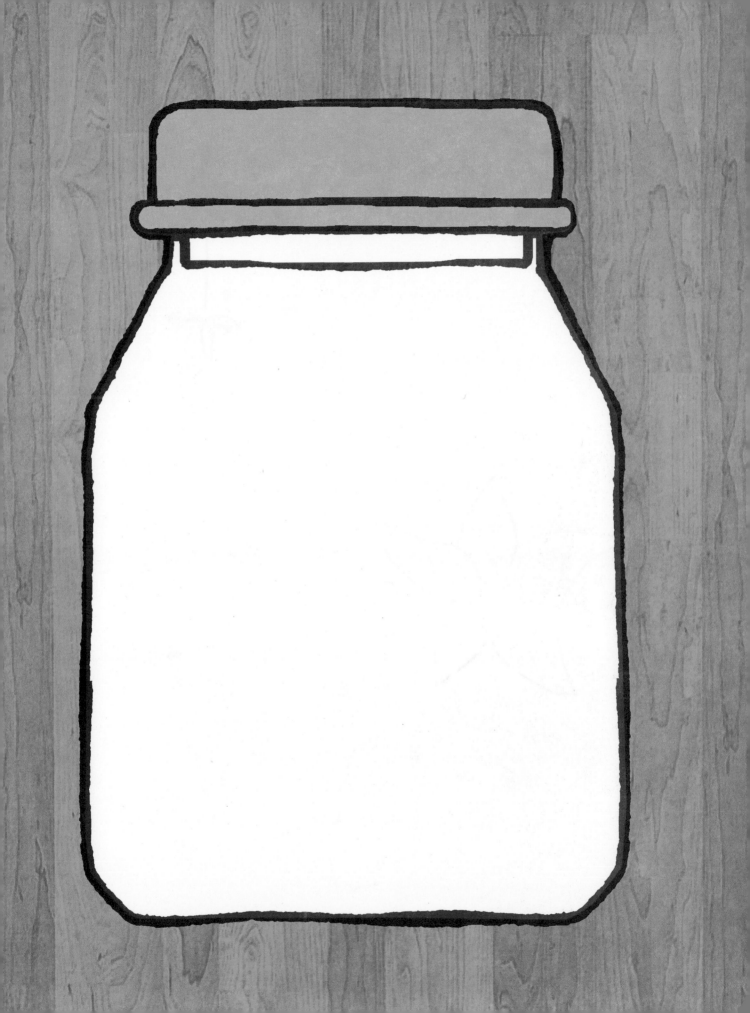

Draw the day you've just had.

Turn these shapes into insects.

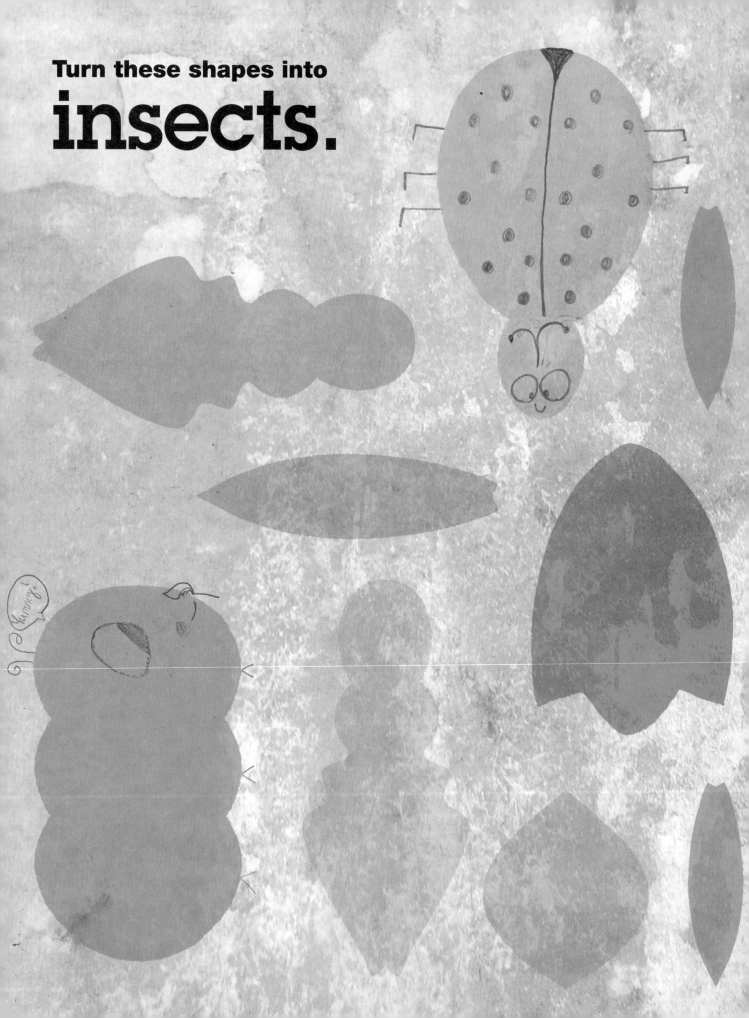

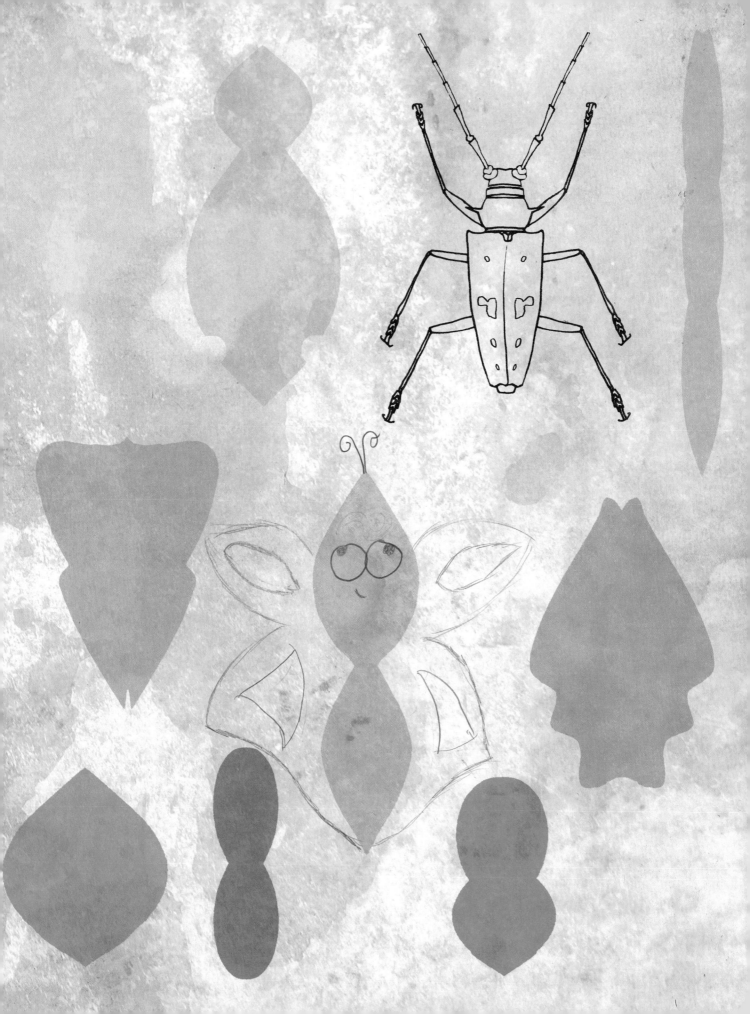

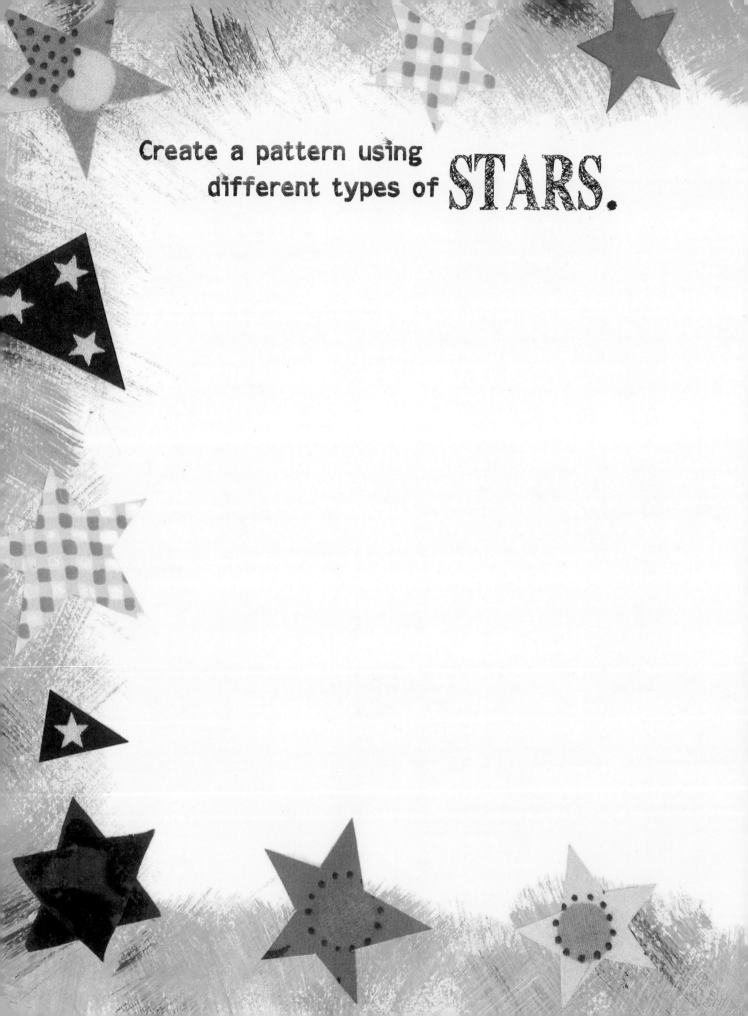

Create a pattern using different types of STARS.

Space for your
creativity.

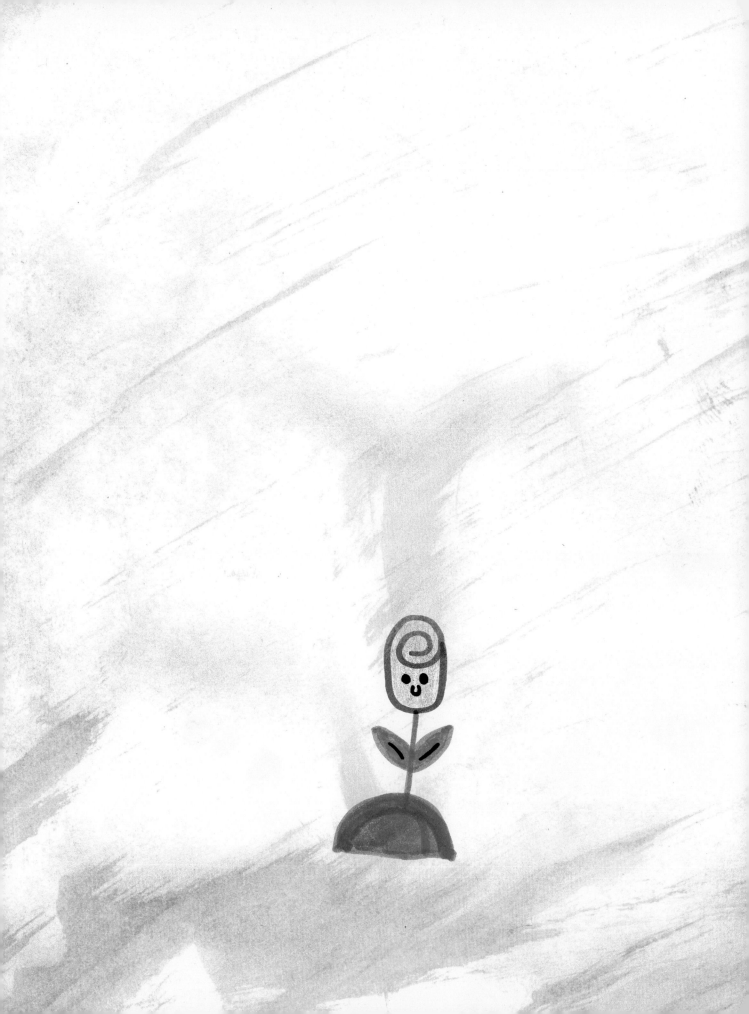

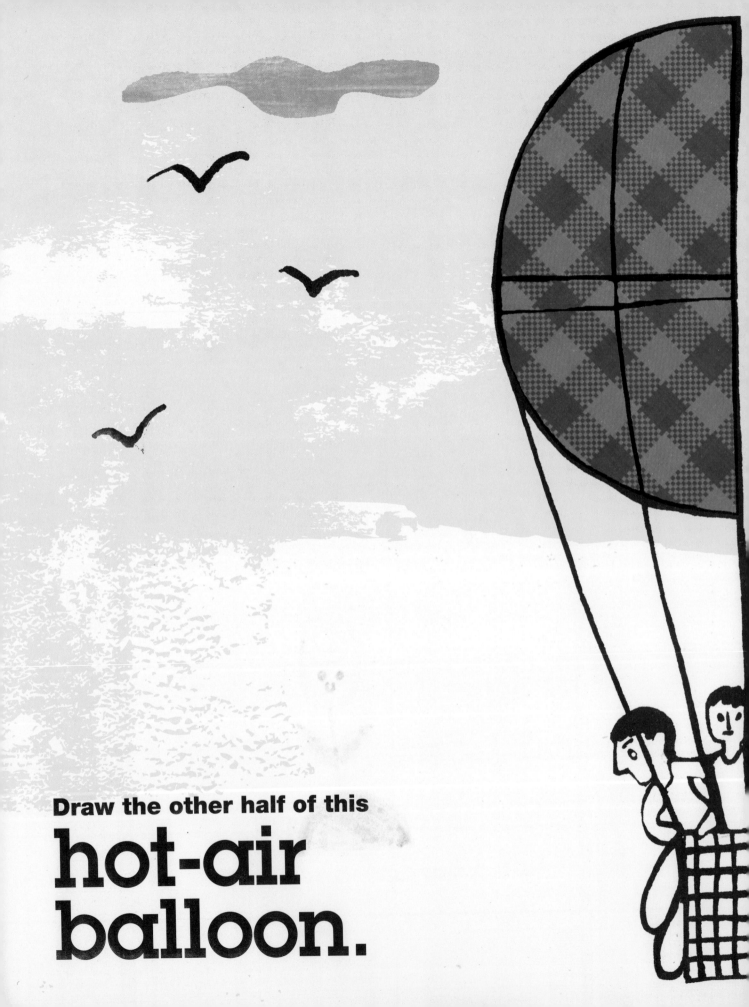

Draw the other half of this

hot-air balloon.

Draw some more
passengers
in the basket.

Draw your favorite BOOK.

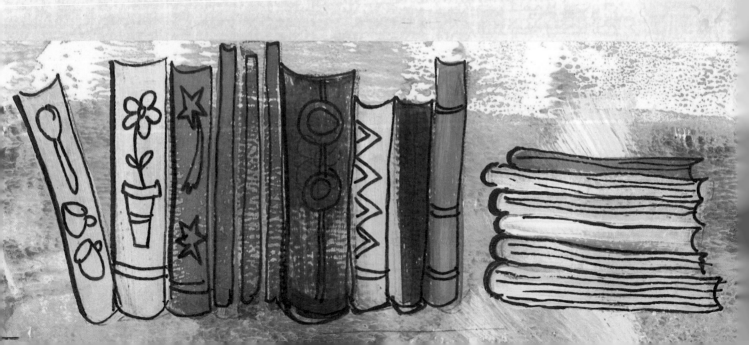

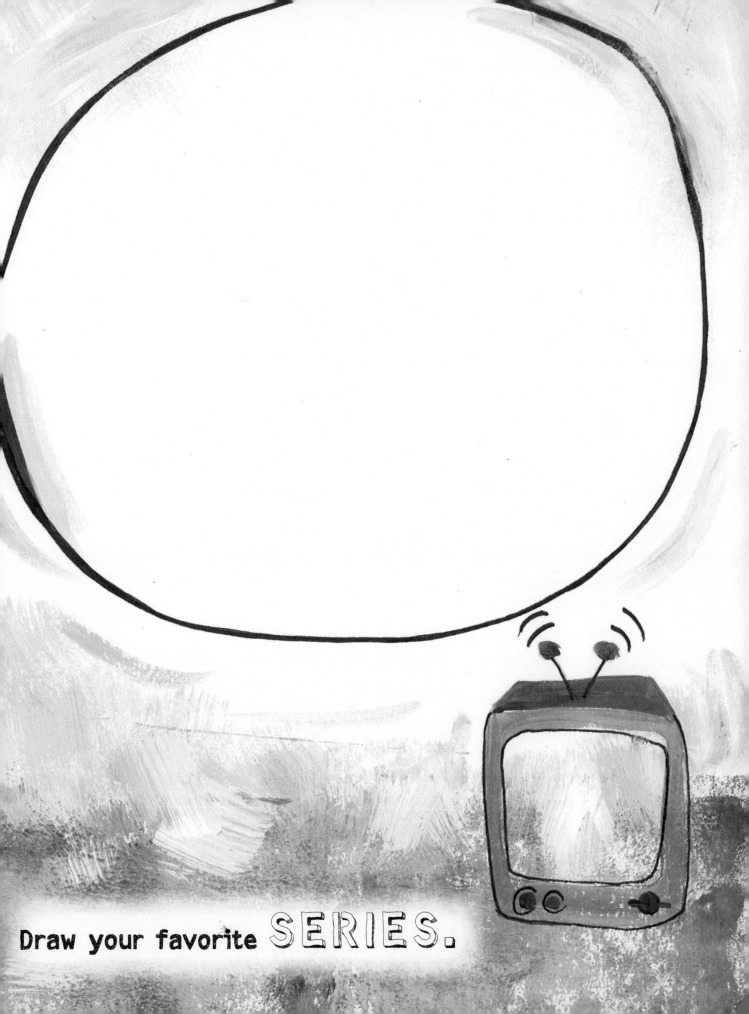

Draw your favorite SERIES.

Create a pattern using
spirals.

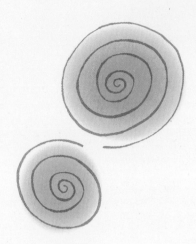

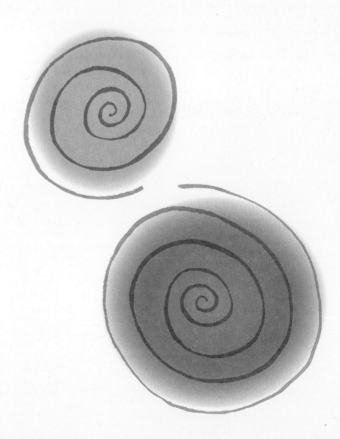

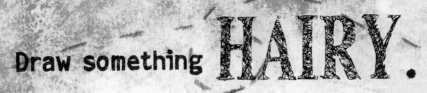

Draw something HAIRY.

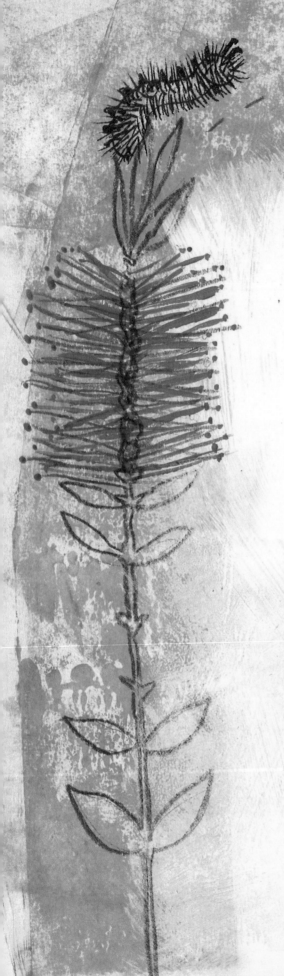

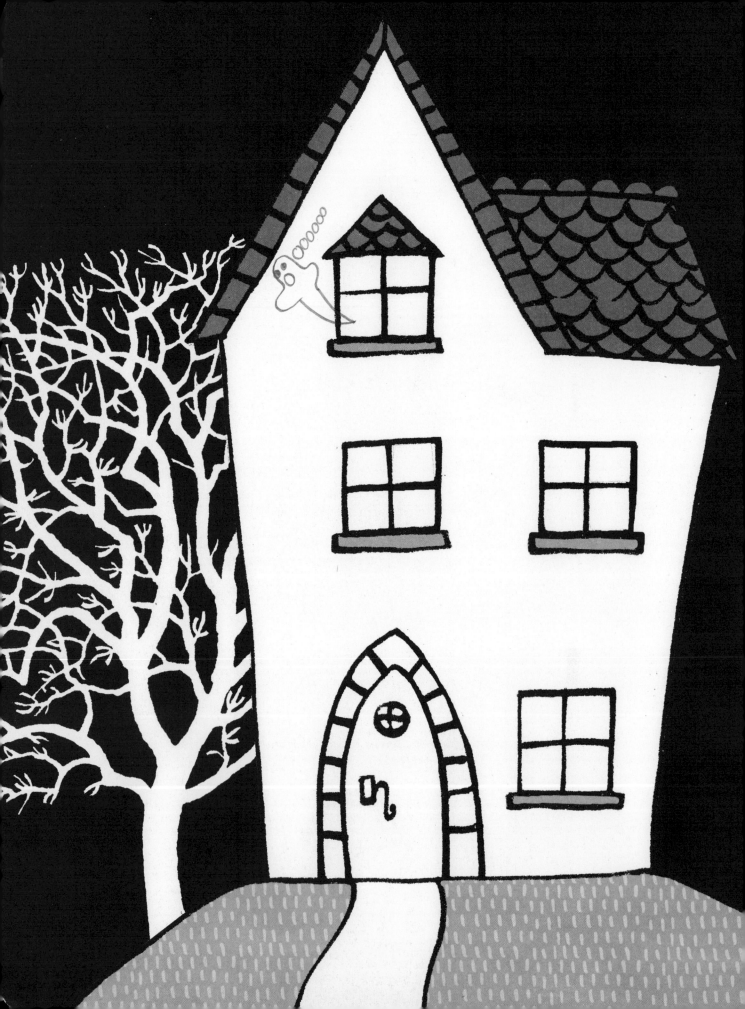

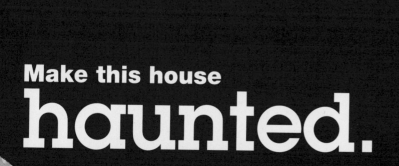

Make this house
haunted.

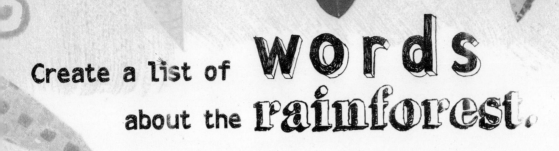

Create a list of **words** about the **rainforest.**

Grow those words into an

image.

Draw your favorite thing

using only your favorite color.

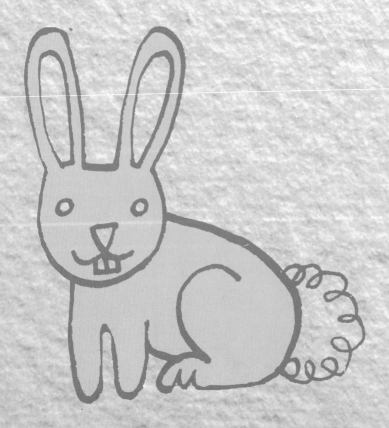

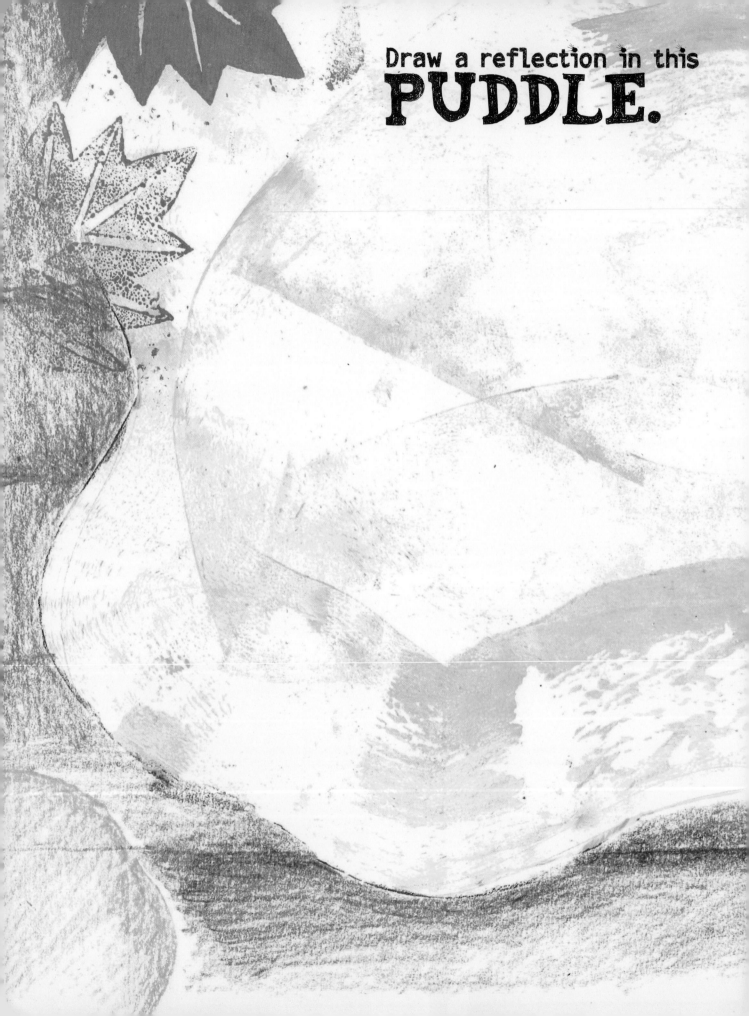

Draw a reflection in this
PUDDLE.

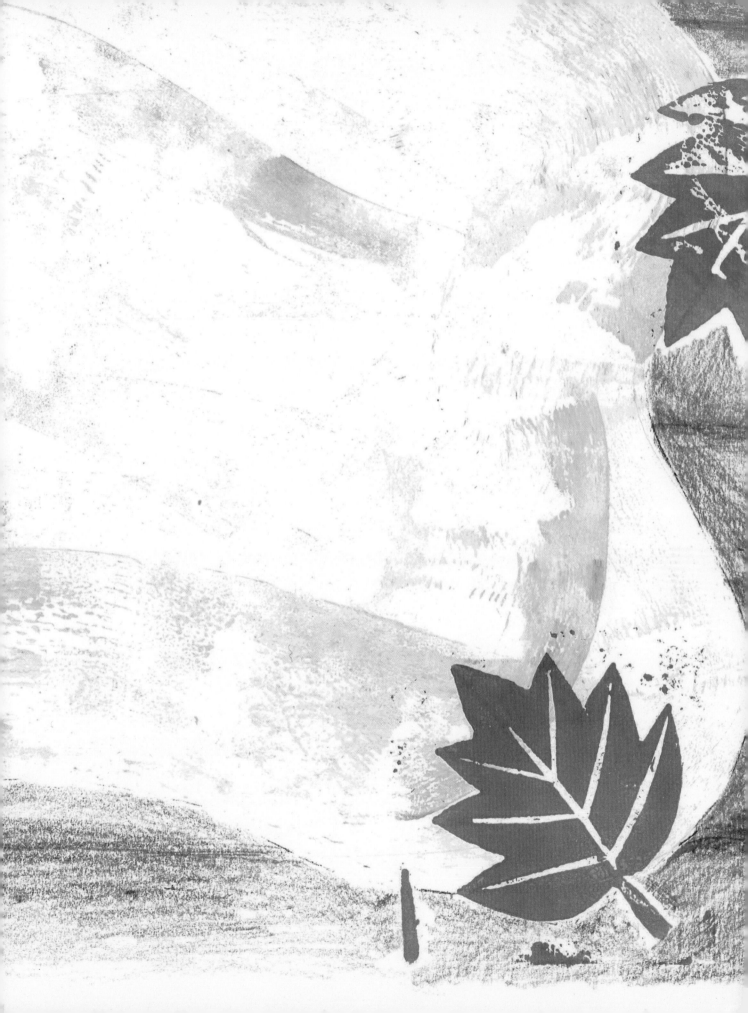

Doodle, color, shade, or scribble anything.

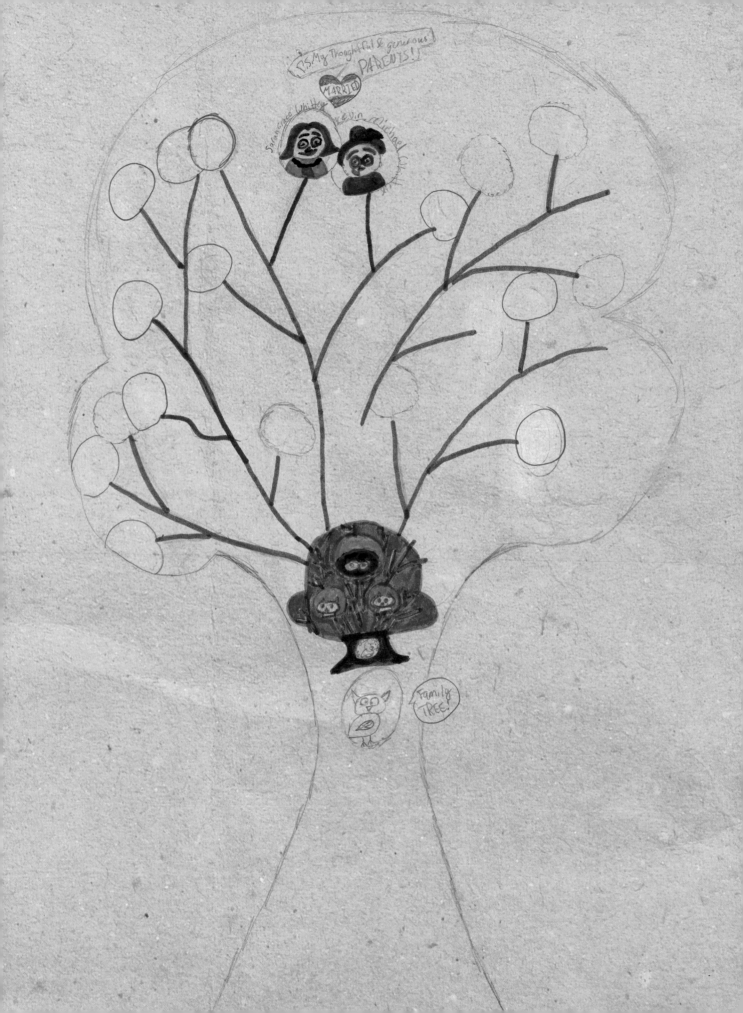

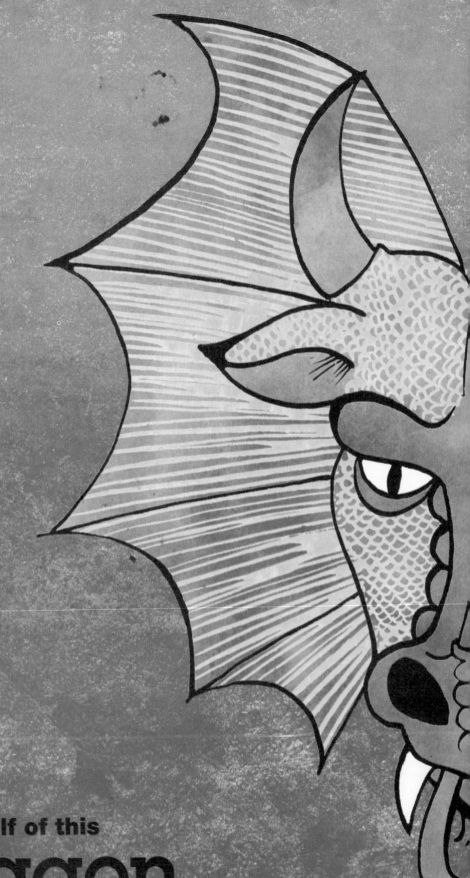

Draw the other half of this

dragon.

Draw a **striped spot.**

Draw a **SPOTTED STRIPE.**

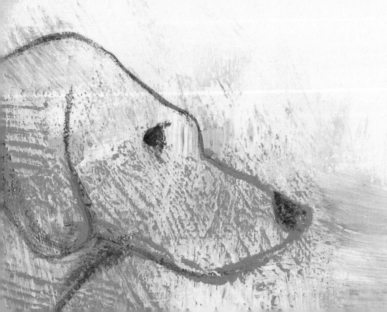

Draw a striped dalmation.

Draw a spotted TIGER.

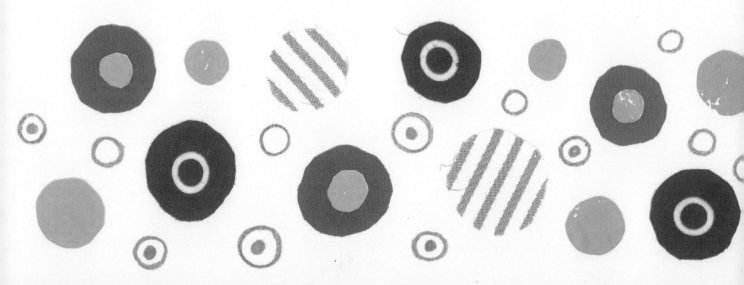

Draw some people in line waiting for the sale to start tomorrow.

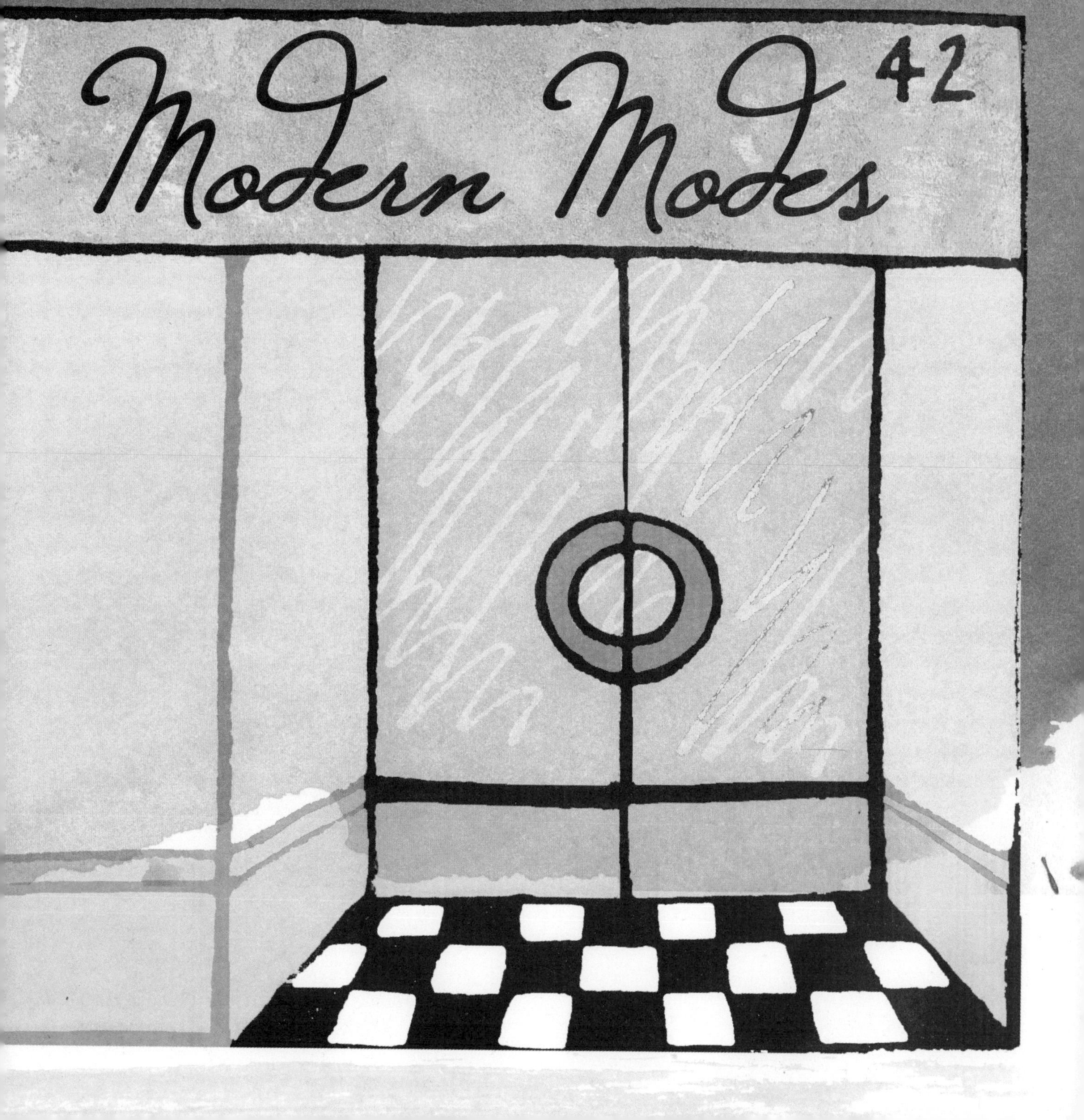
Modern Modes
42

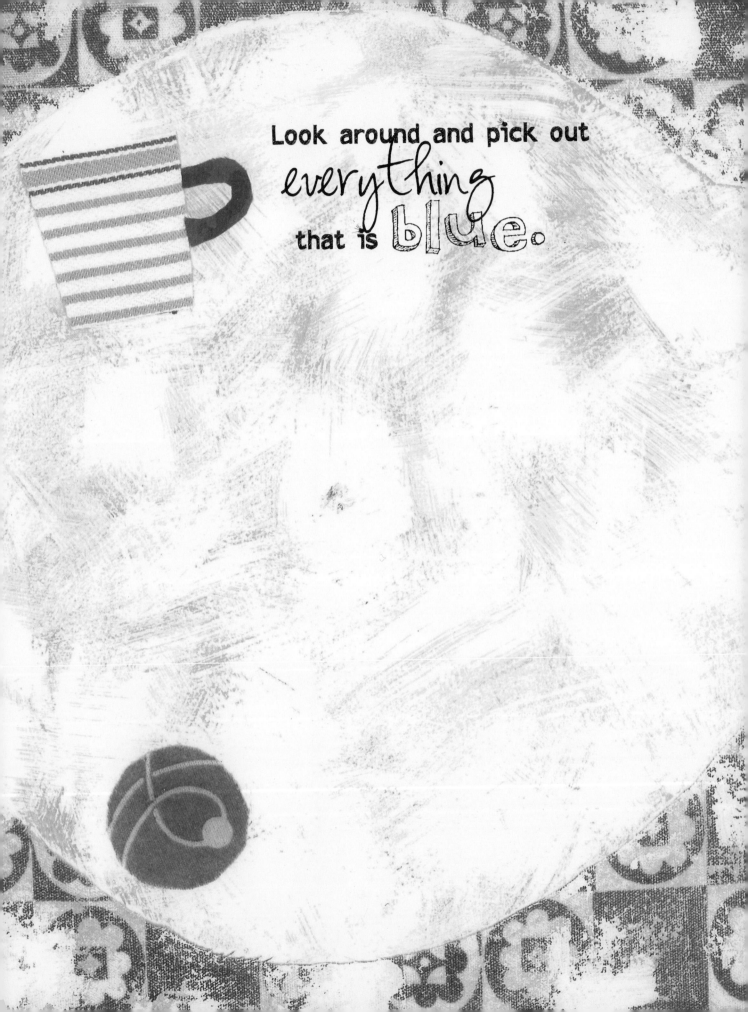

Look around and pick out
everything
that is blue.

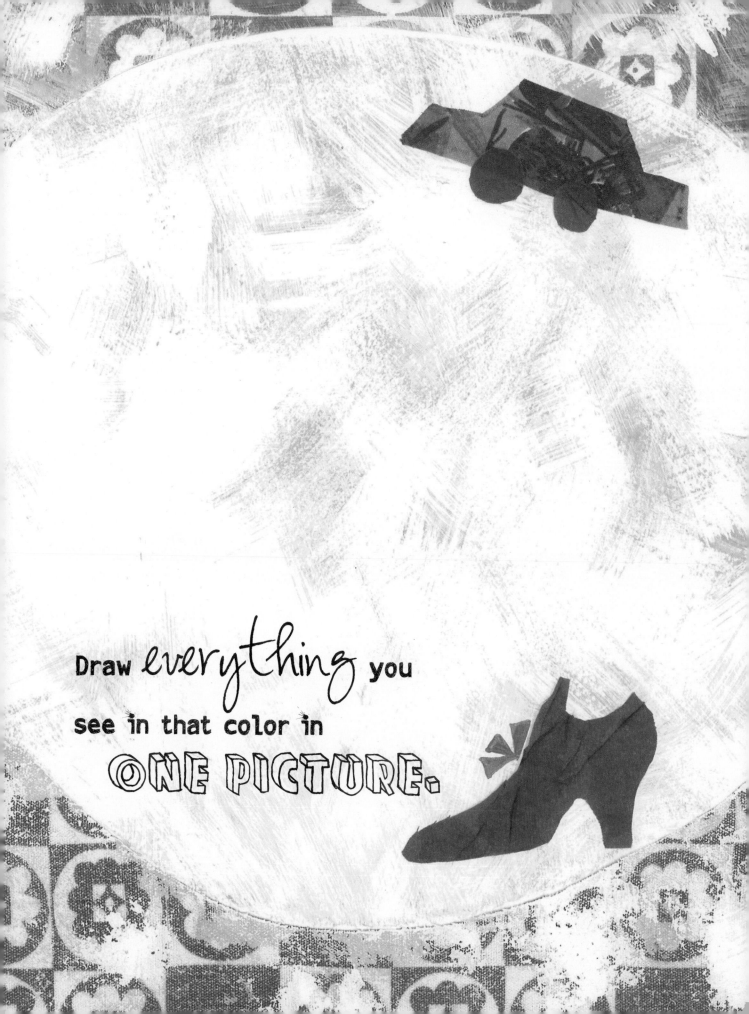

Draw *everything* you see in that color in ONE PICTURE.

Draw **wings** for yourself and your best friend and **fly away.**

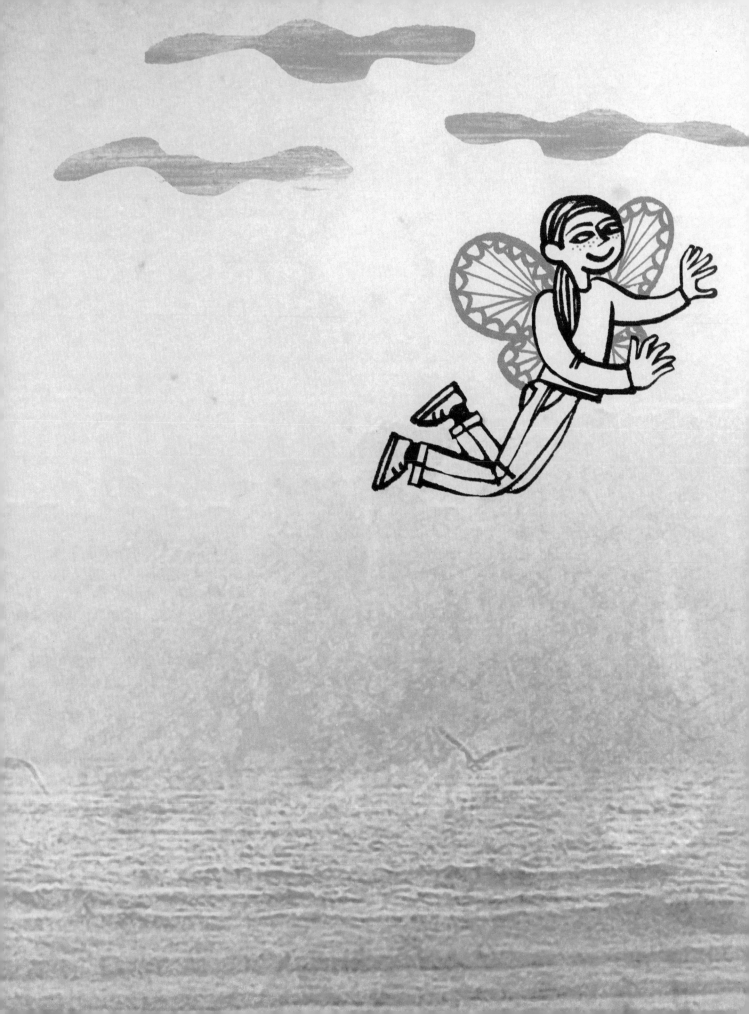

Draw a *windy day.*

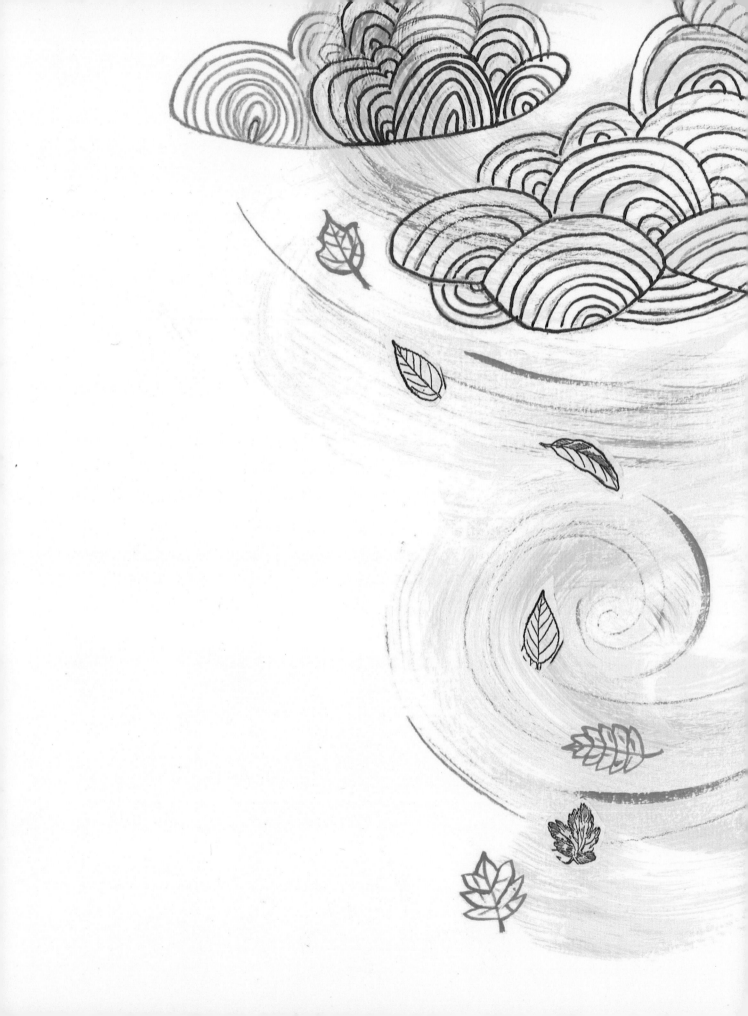

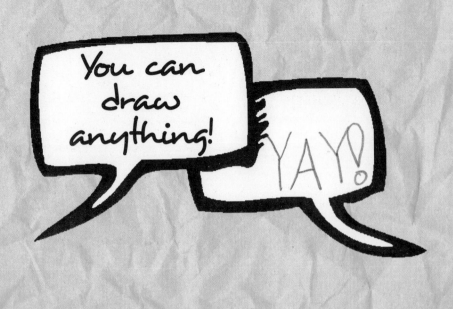

Draw something **WIDE.**

Draw something NARROW.

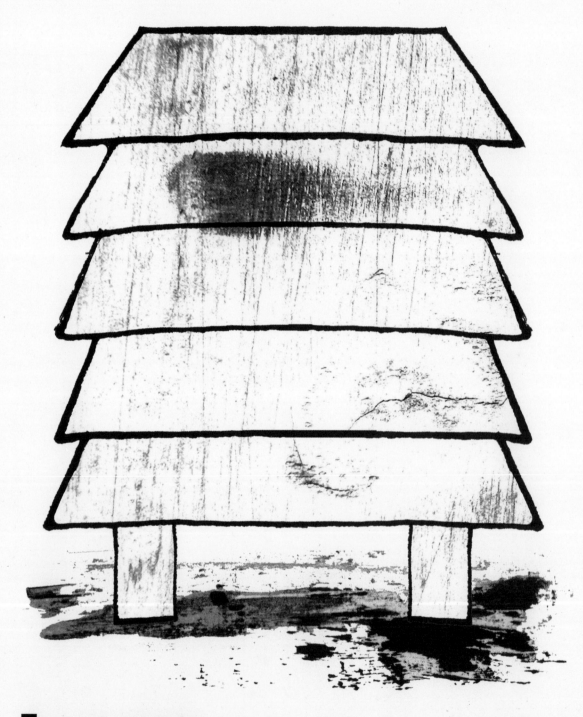

Add **bees** to this beehive.

Plant flowers

for these bees.

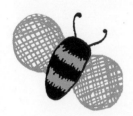

"Think left and and think low Oh, the thinks up if only you

think right
and think high.
you can think
try. "   Dr. Seuss.

Create a **pattern** using only
the letters from your name, over and over.

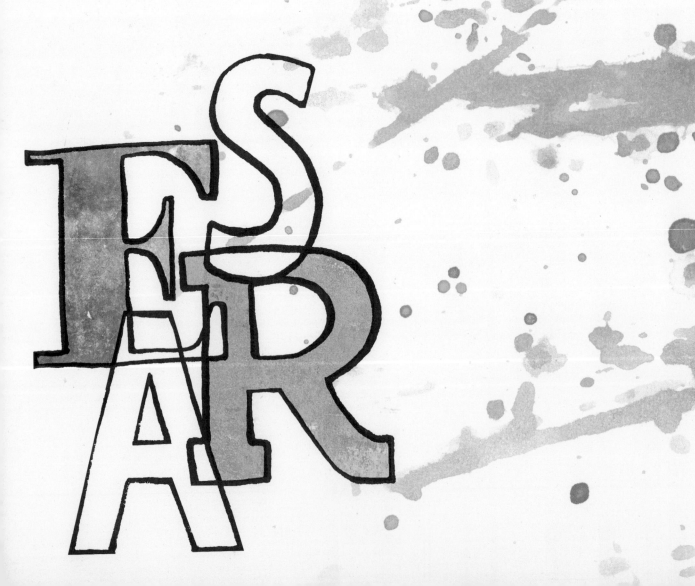

Draw a
DIAMOND
spinning.

Draw a ZIGZAG waving.

Draw a **triangle**
doing cartwheels.

Draw a **GEOMETRIC**
TESSELLATING pattern.

Fill this **seabed**
with things that can **swim.**

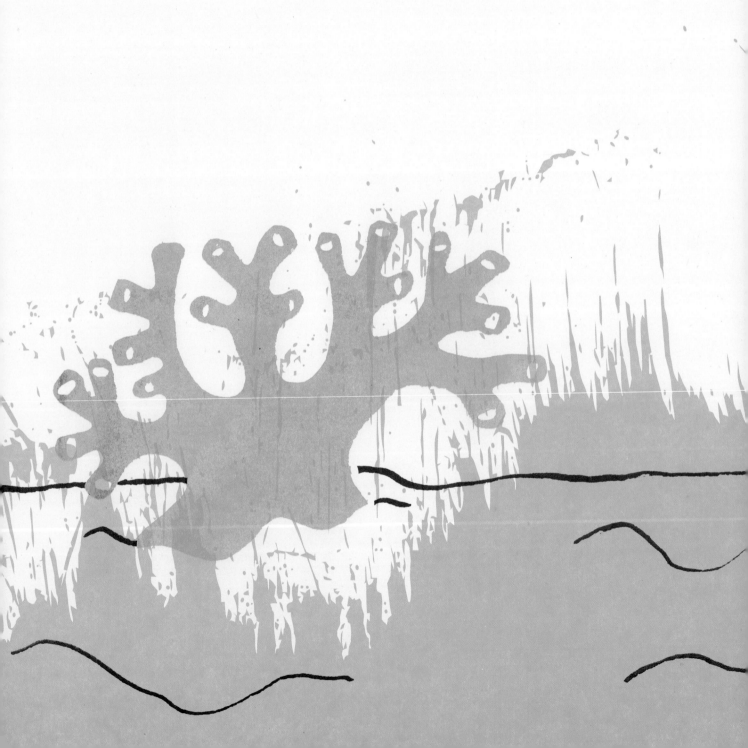

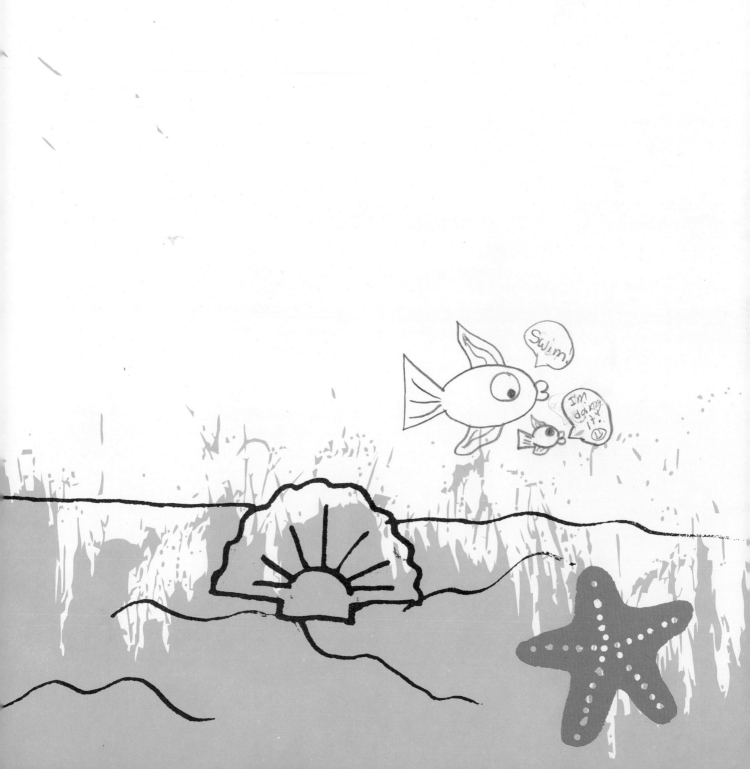

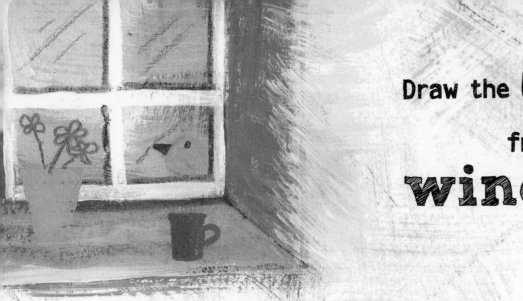

Draw the *view* from your **window.**

Draw the view from **OUTSIDE** your window **looking in.**

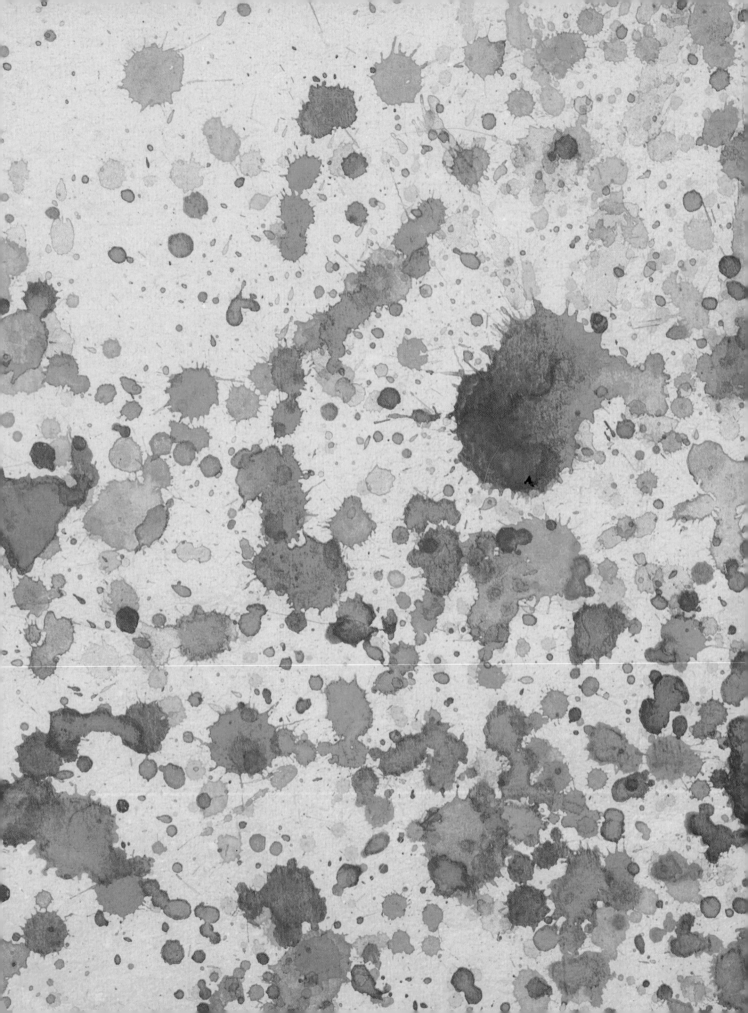

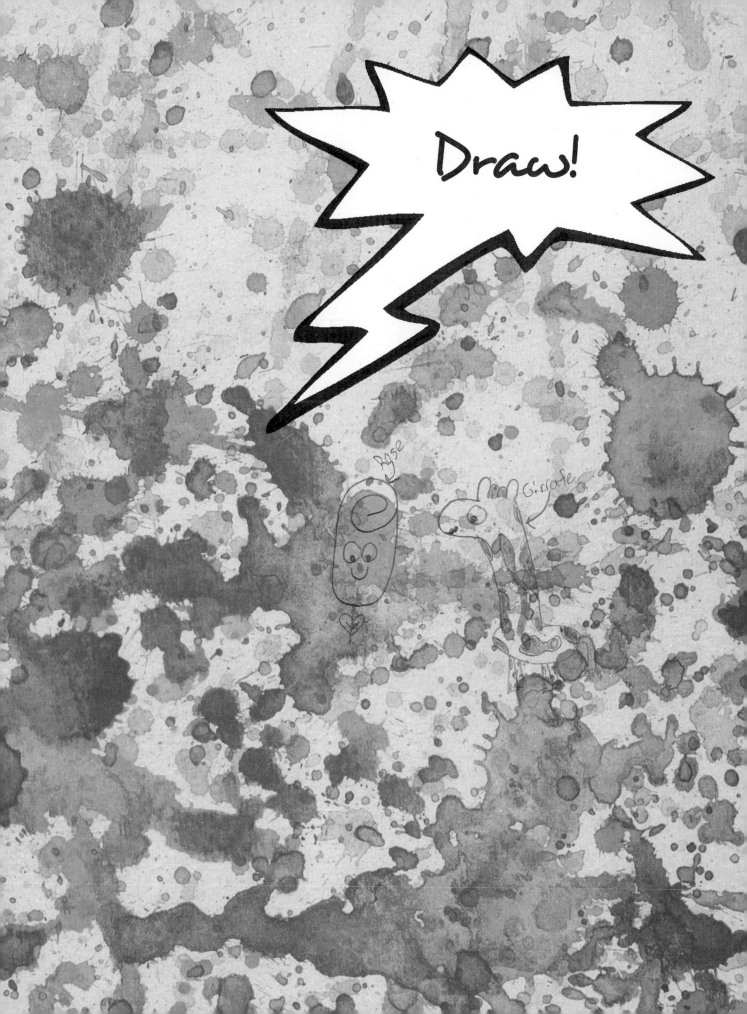

Design these curtains.

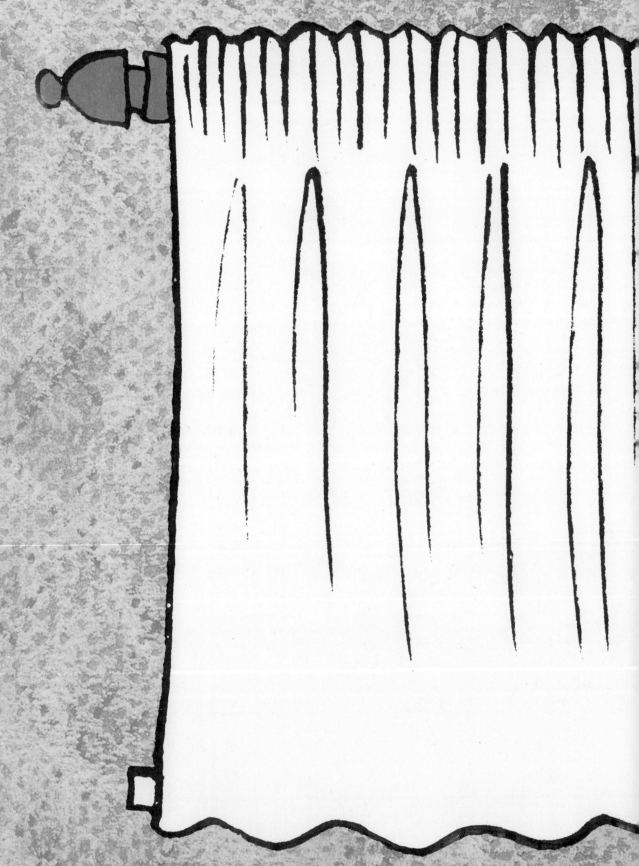

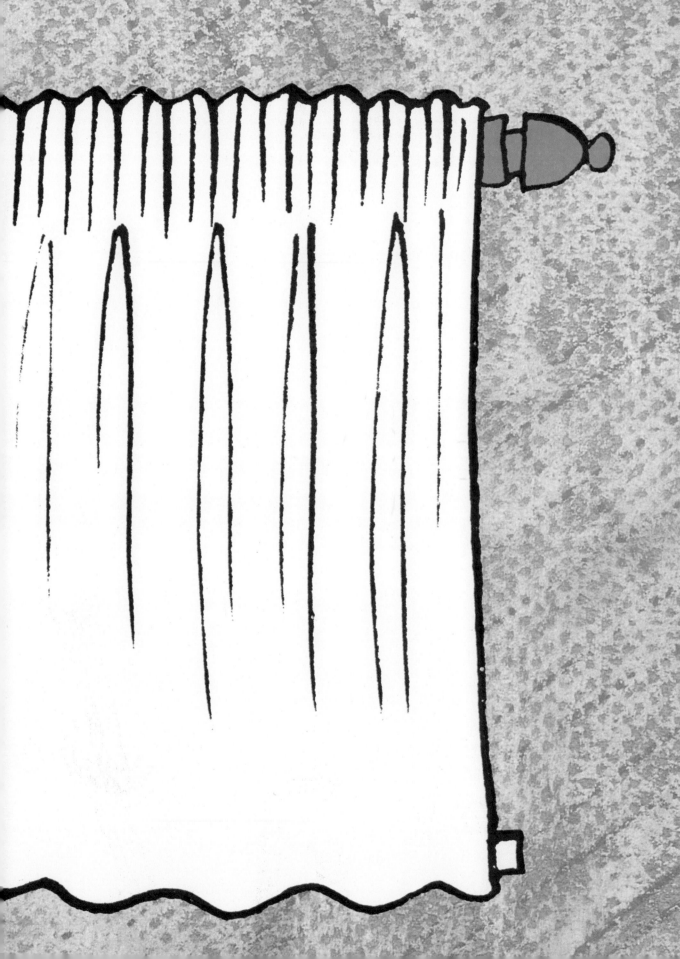

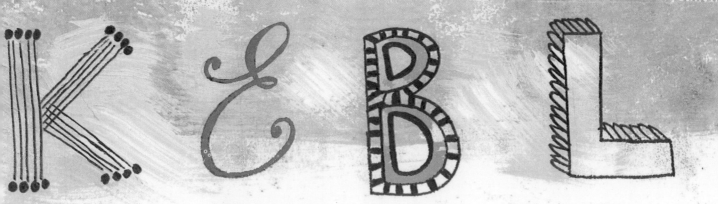

Create a new **font** that shows your *personal* style.

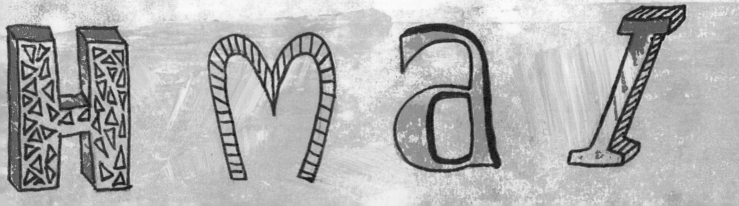

C O T J

Y f S X

Draw a **bicycle** for this dog.

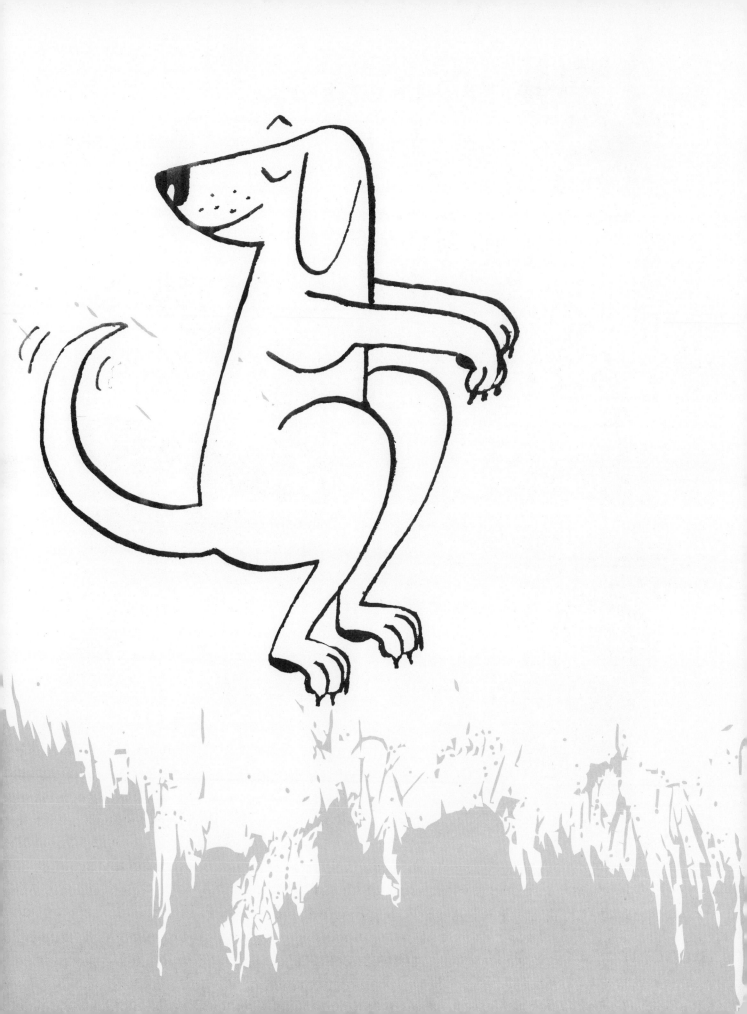

Assign MOODS to each color.

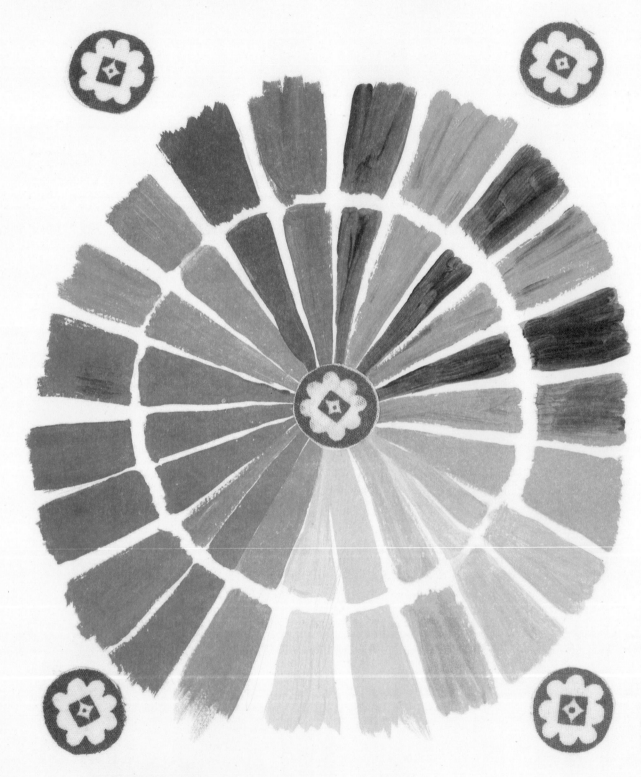

If you **INVERT** these what would
happen to the mood of a picture?

"I've been 40 years discovering that the queen of all colors was black."

Pierre-Auguste Renoir.

Spread your favorite toppings on these bagels.

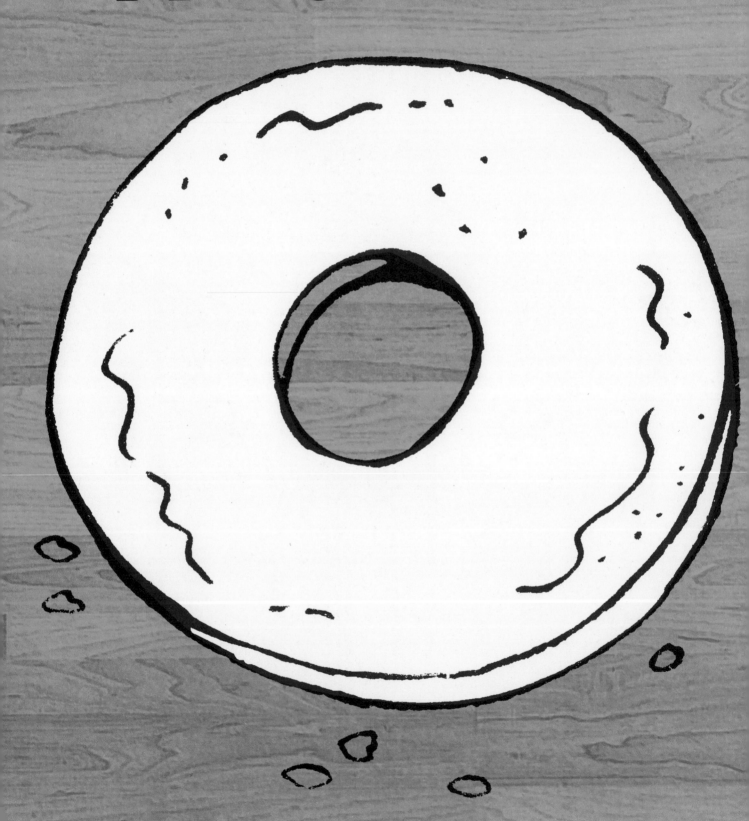

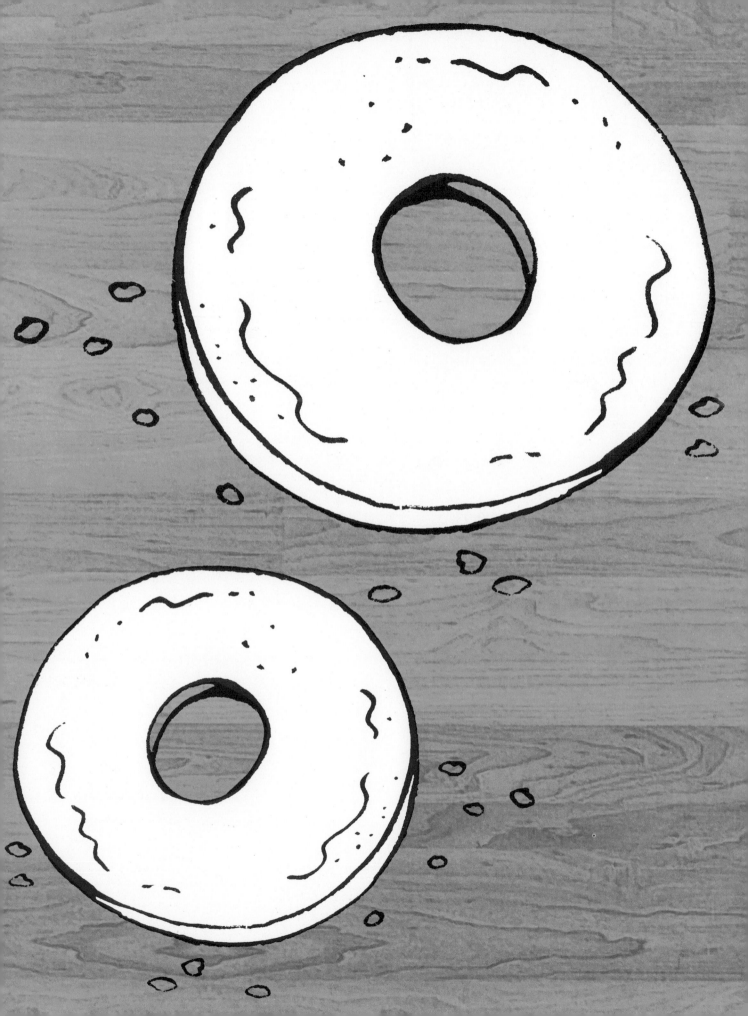

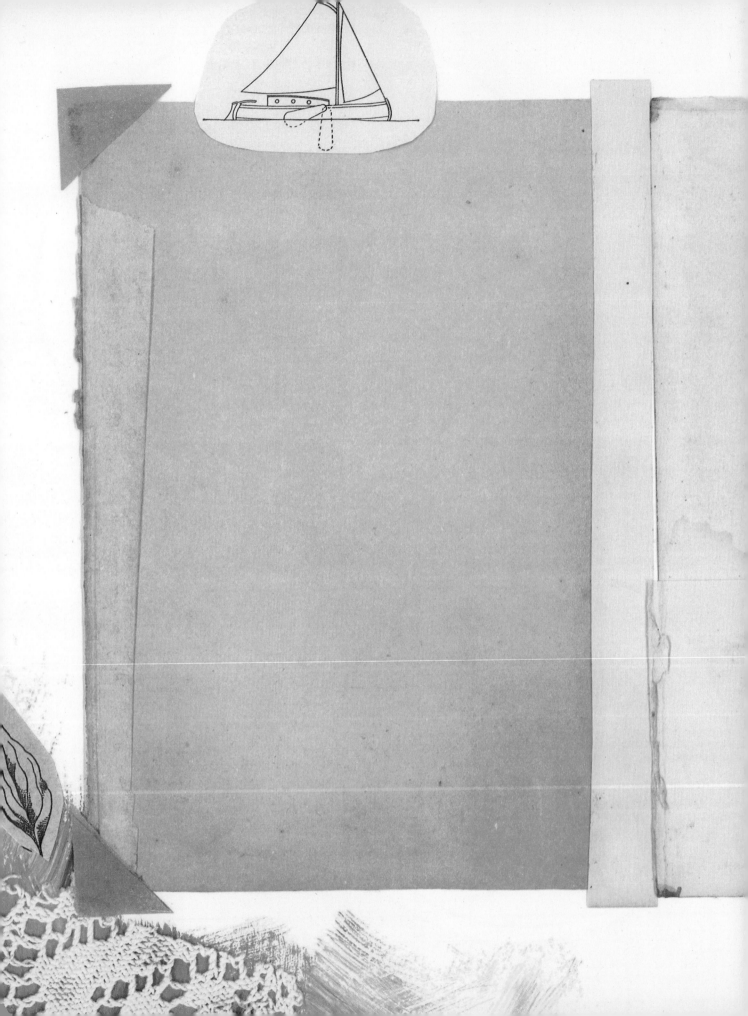

Draw your **happiest** memory.

Getting
Ninja!

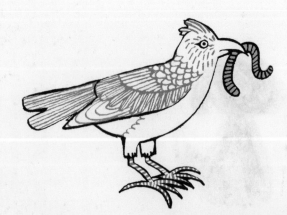

Fill this page with animals that come out in the daytime.

Fill this page with animals that come out at **nighttime.**

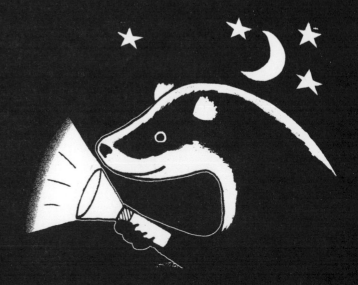

Draw something shiny.

Mr. Sunshine

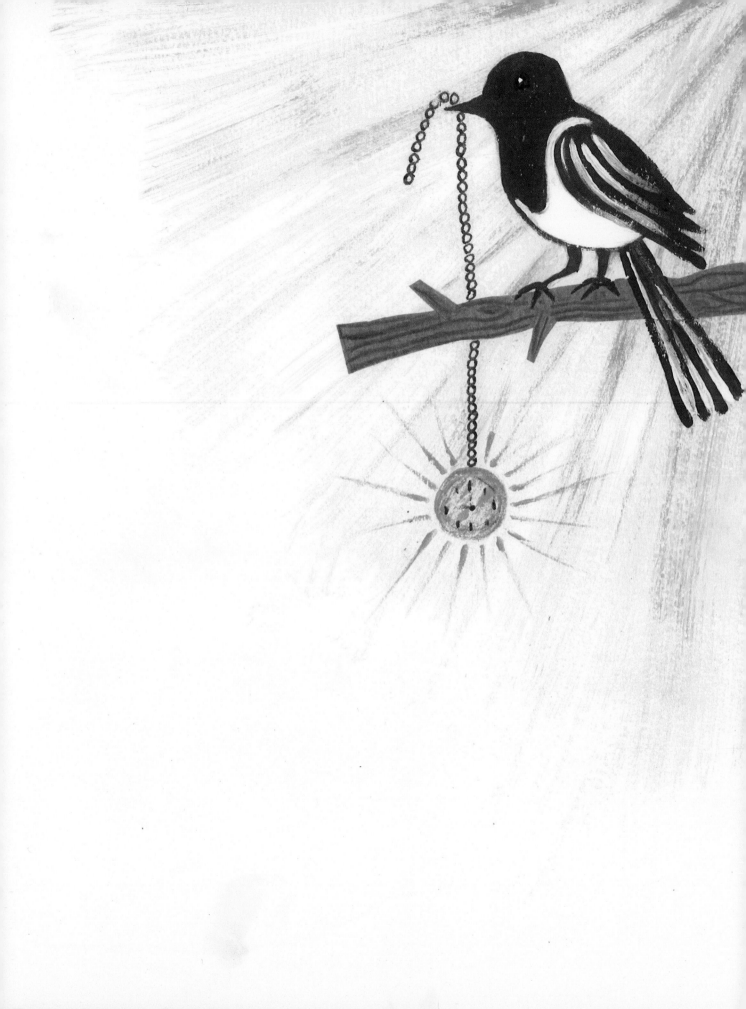

Color these
high heels.

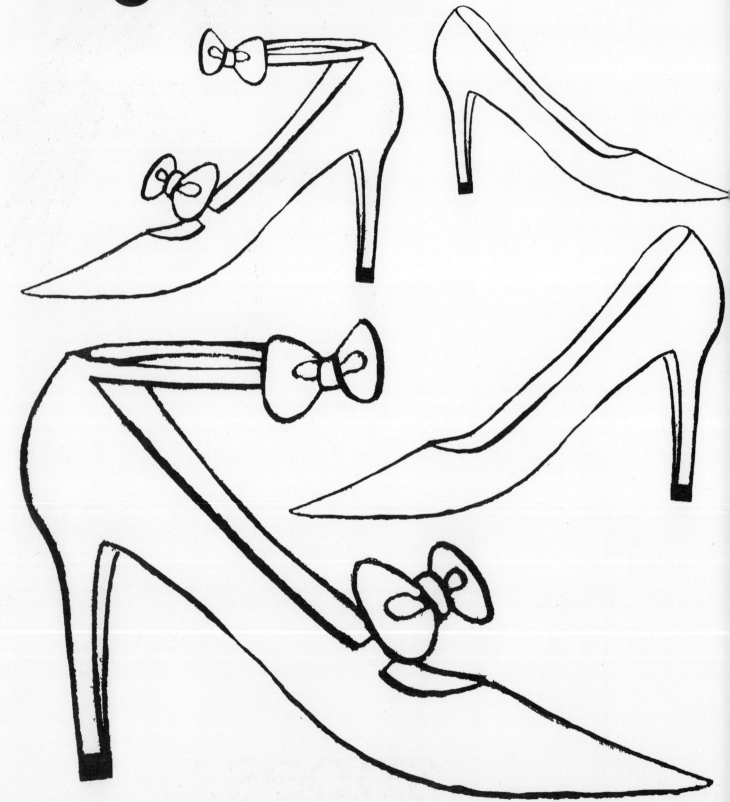

Now design your own shoes.

Add a row of **exotic birds**
to this branch in **BLACK AND WHITE.**

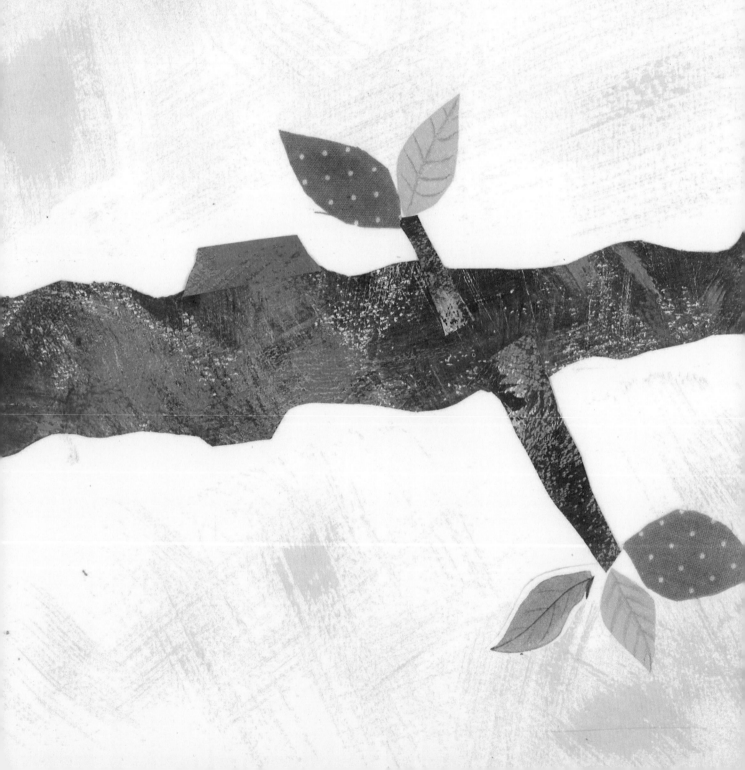

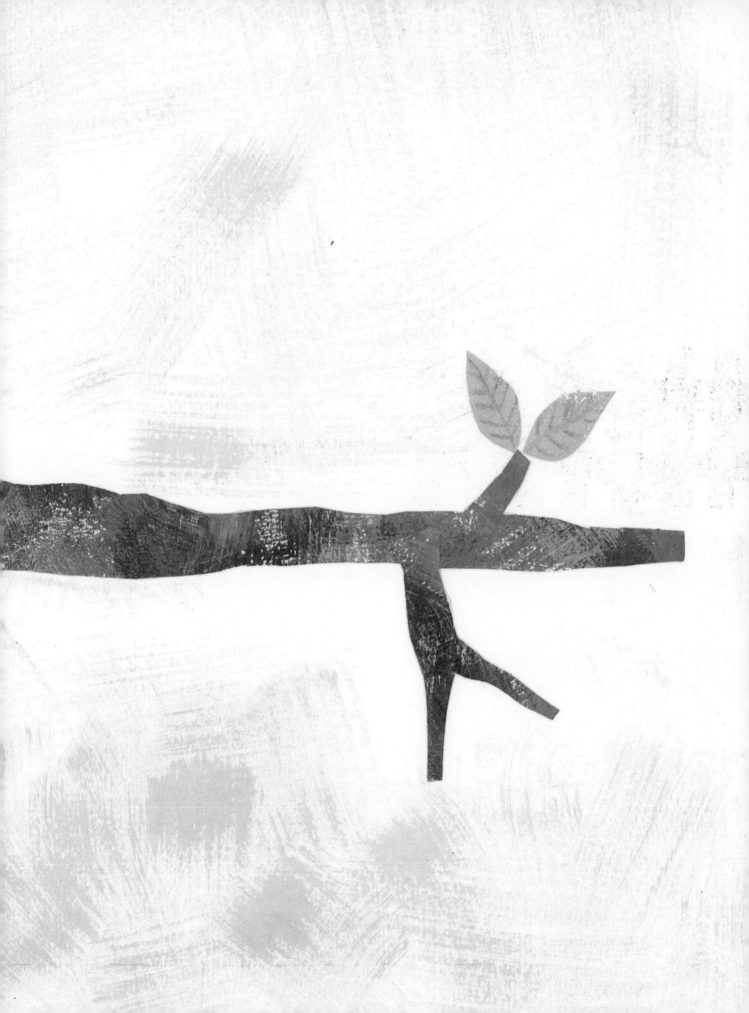

Draw...

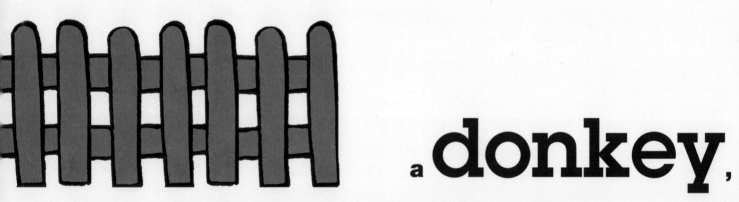

ₐdonkey,

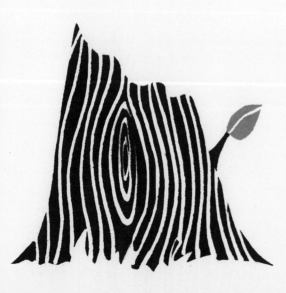

ₐbear,

and a
hippo.

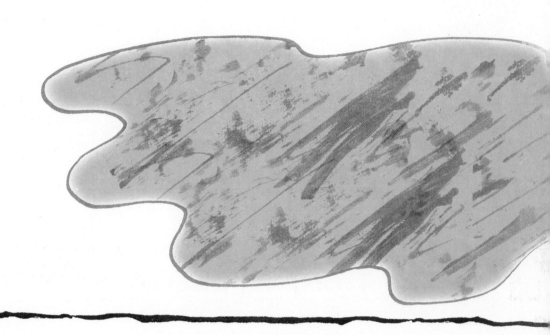

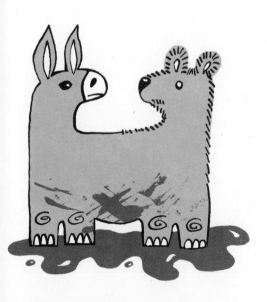

**Now draw one
image of all three.**

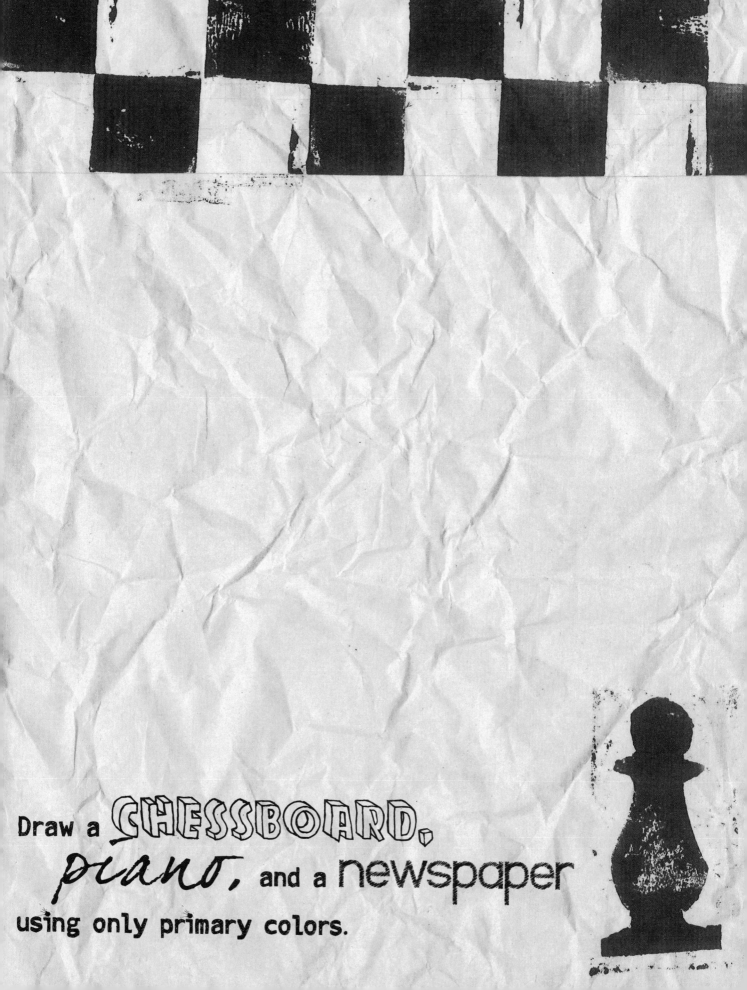

Draw a **CHESSBOARD**, *piano,* and a newspaper using only primary colors.

Draw a staircase

using only WAVY LINES.

Draw the **OCEAN** using only diagonal lines.

Draw an alien **spaceship.**

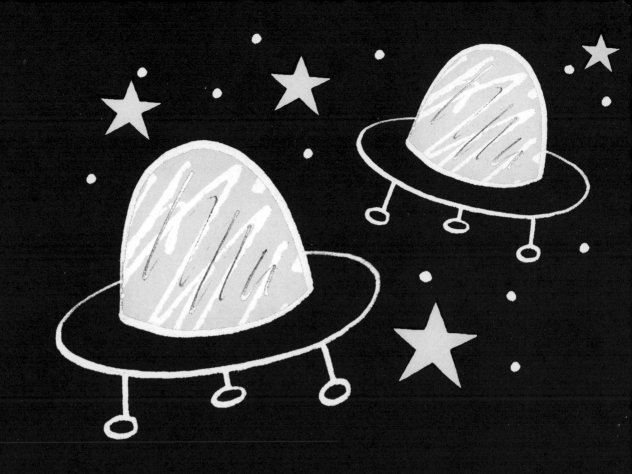

Draw what's **directly in front** of you using one continuous line.

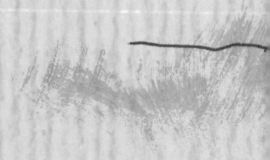

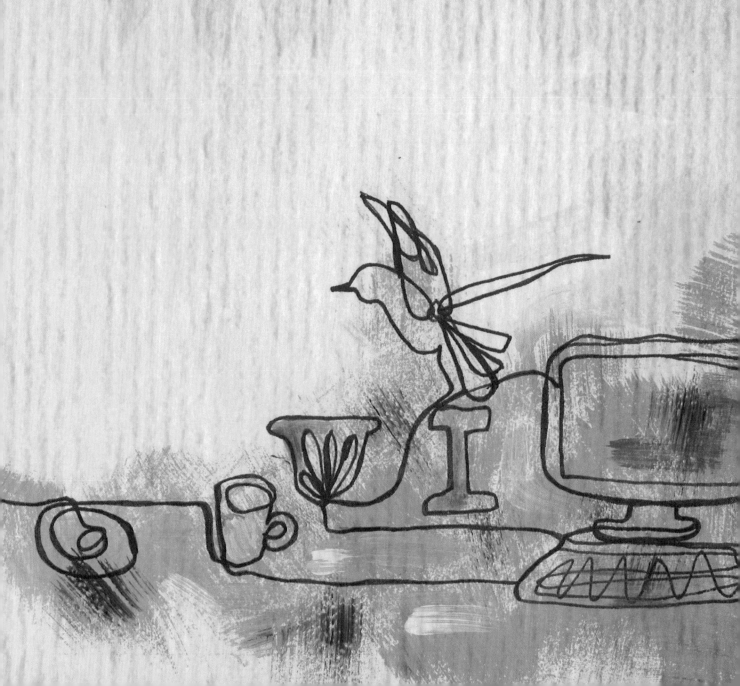

Fill this page with
rectangles.

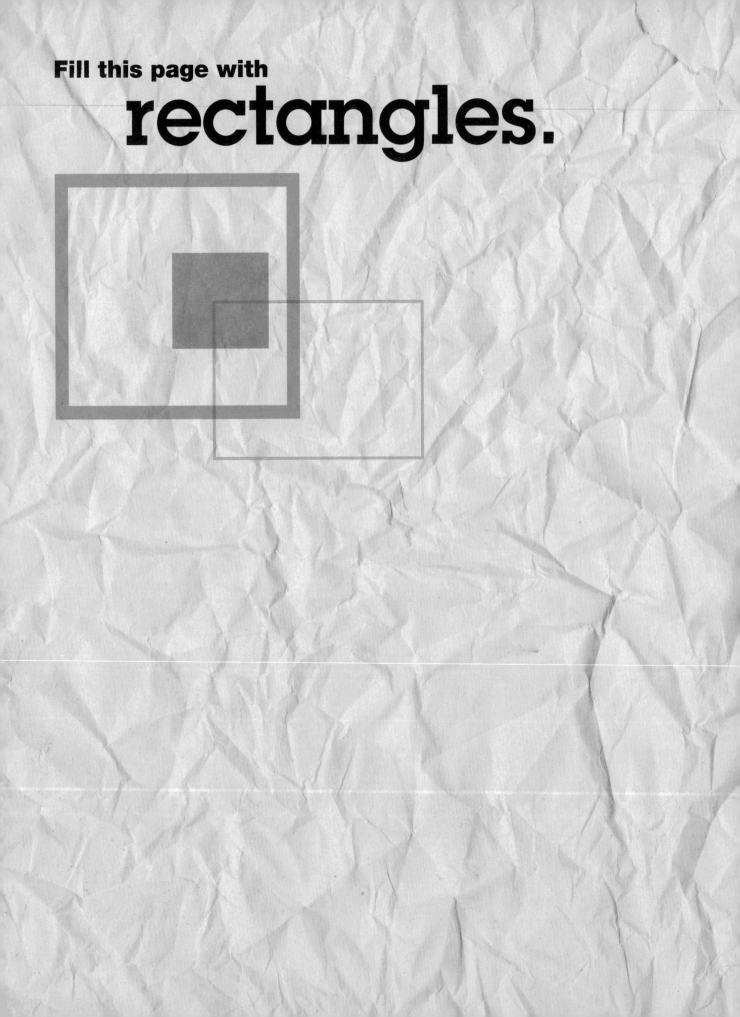

**Can you turn those
rectangles into a
family.**

Add dogs

to these collars.

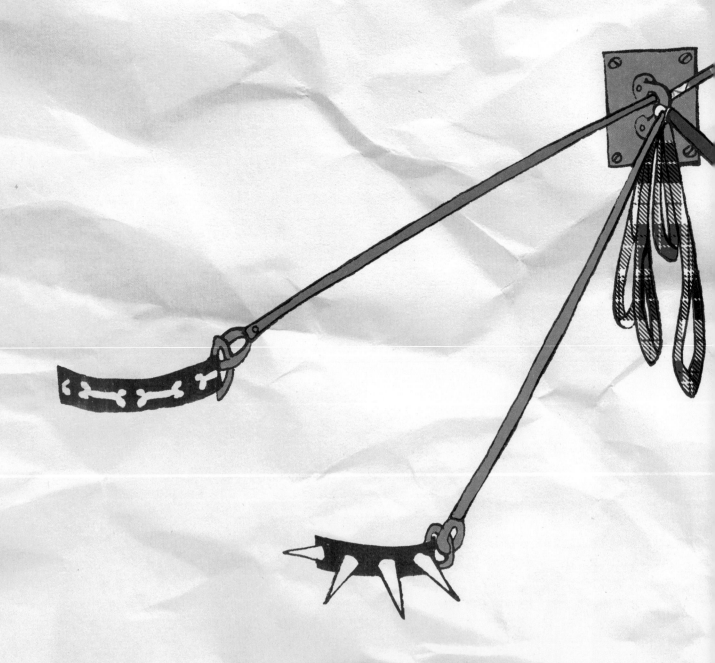

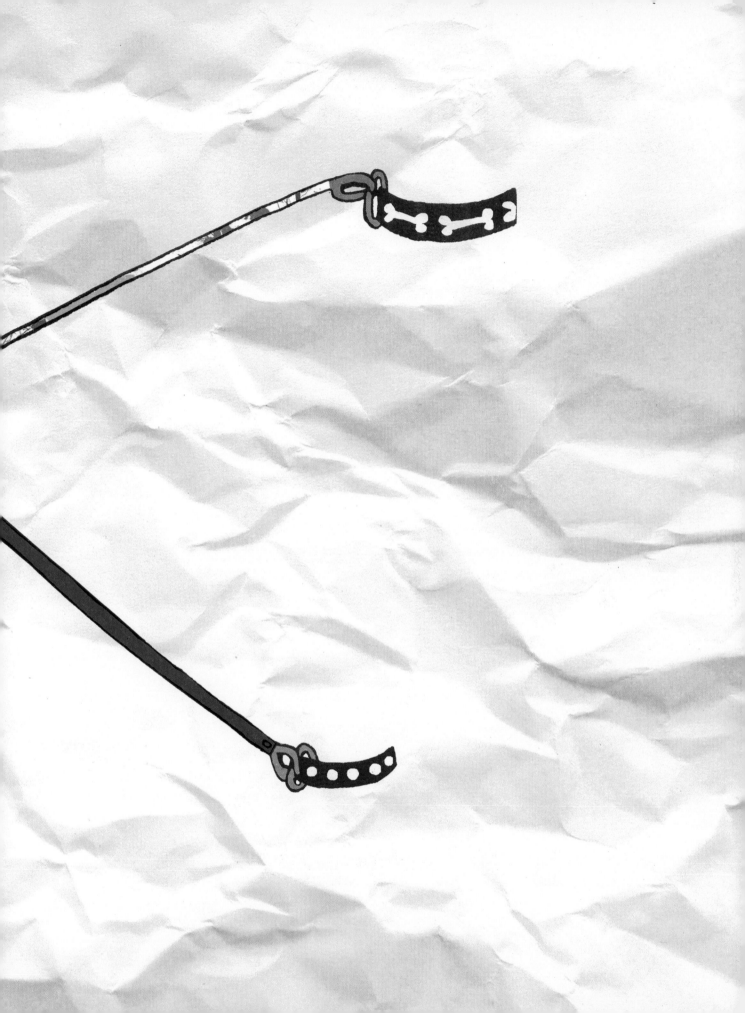

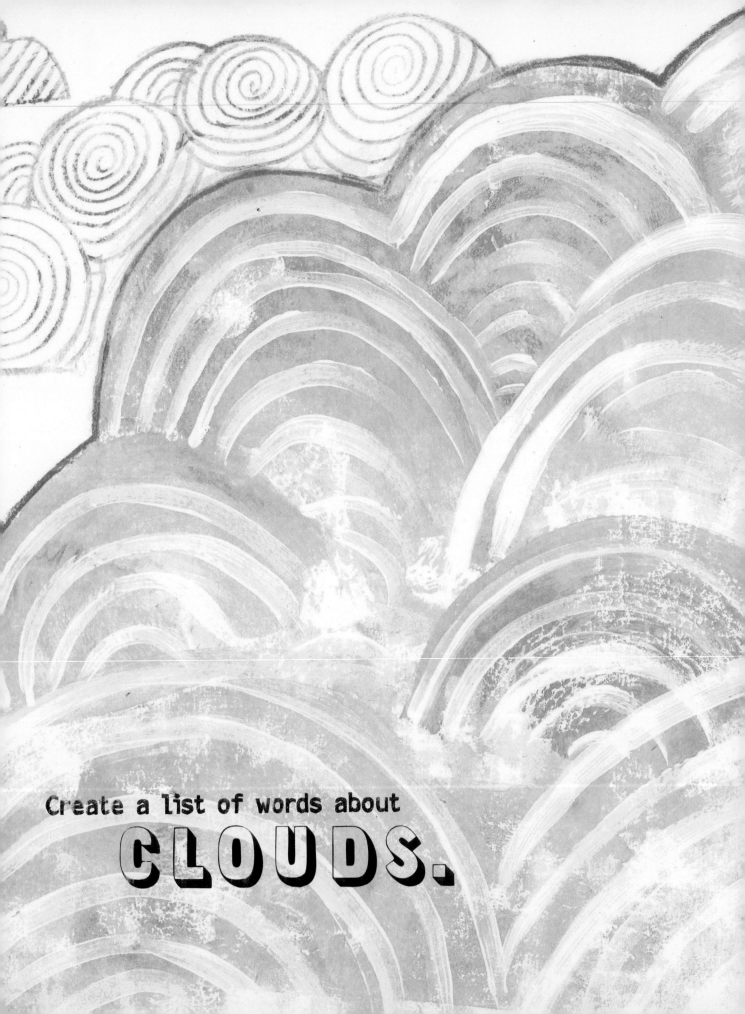

Create a list of words about
CLOUDS.

Float

those words into an image.

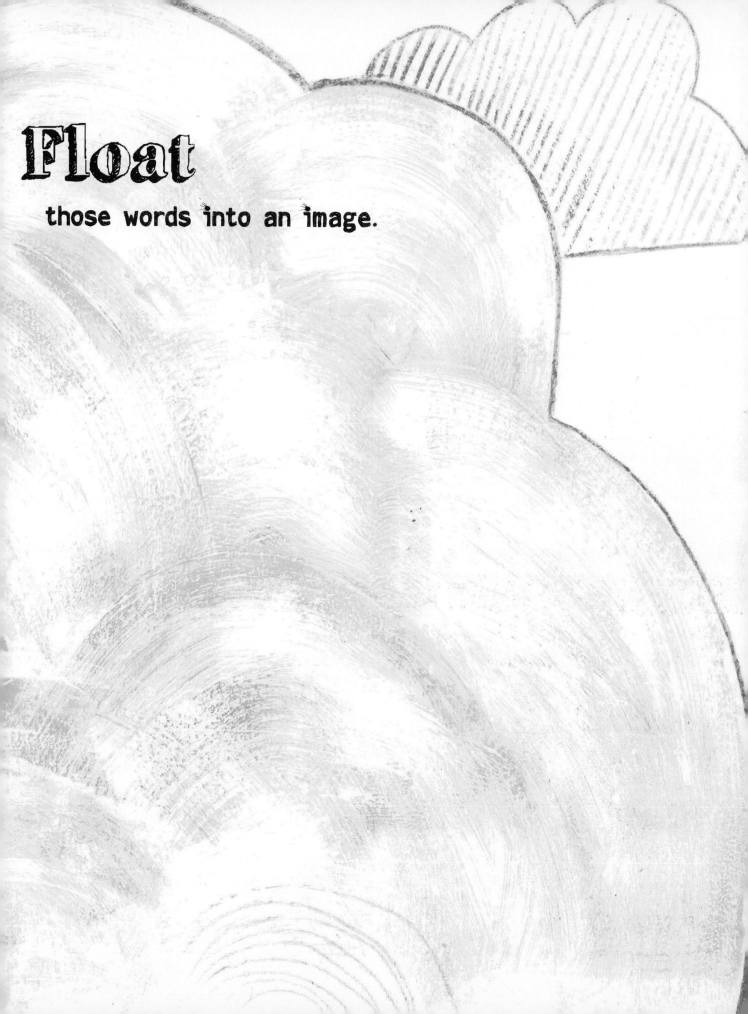

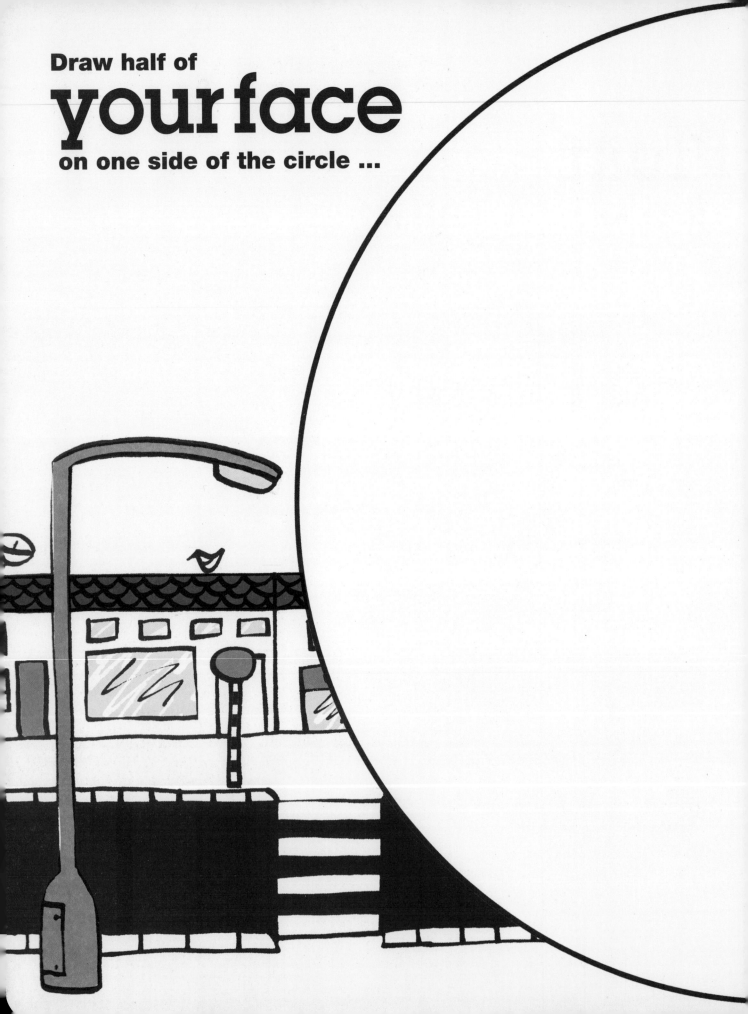

Draw half of
your face
on one side of the circle ...

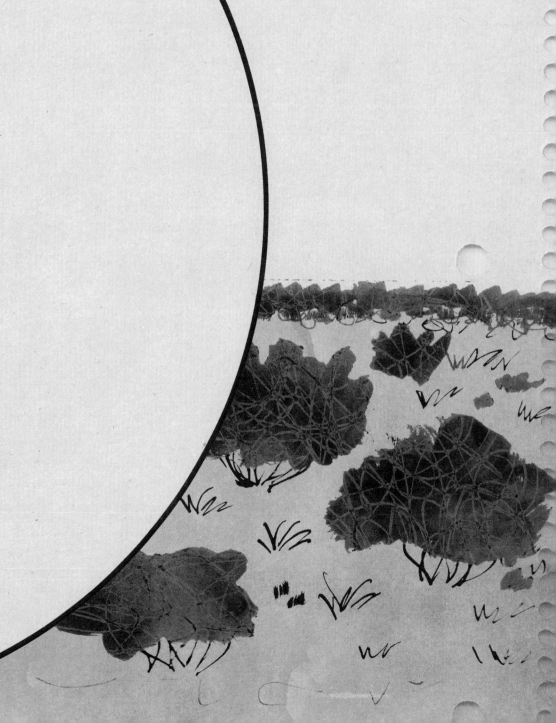

... and draw half of a
lion's face
on the other side.

Draw an **ANT** the size of a house.

Draw an **oak tree**

the size of a grass seed.

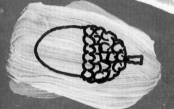
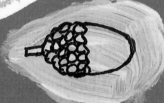

Save everything that is **falling.**

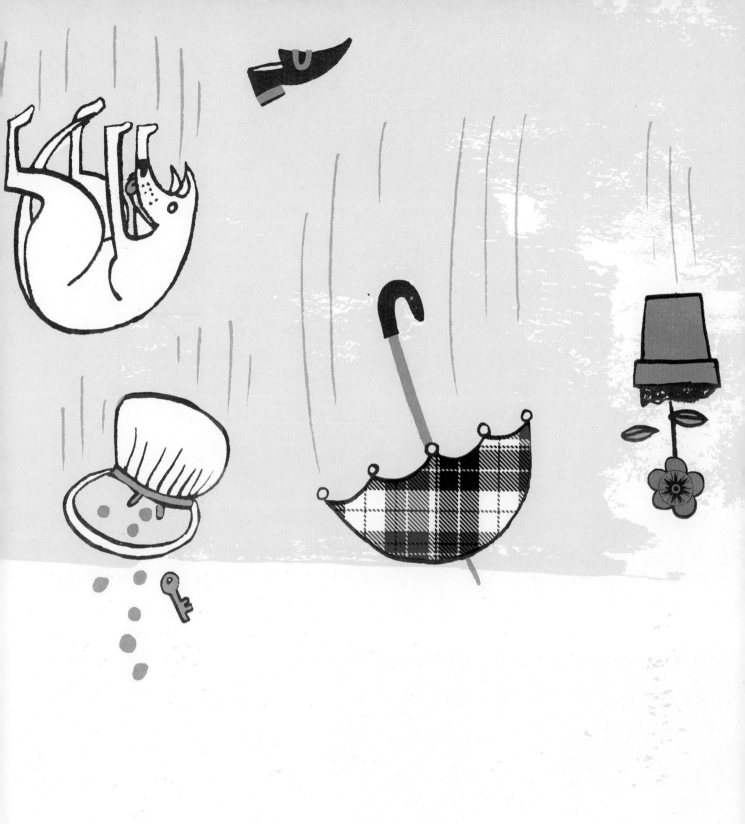

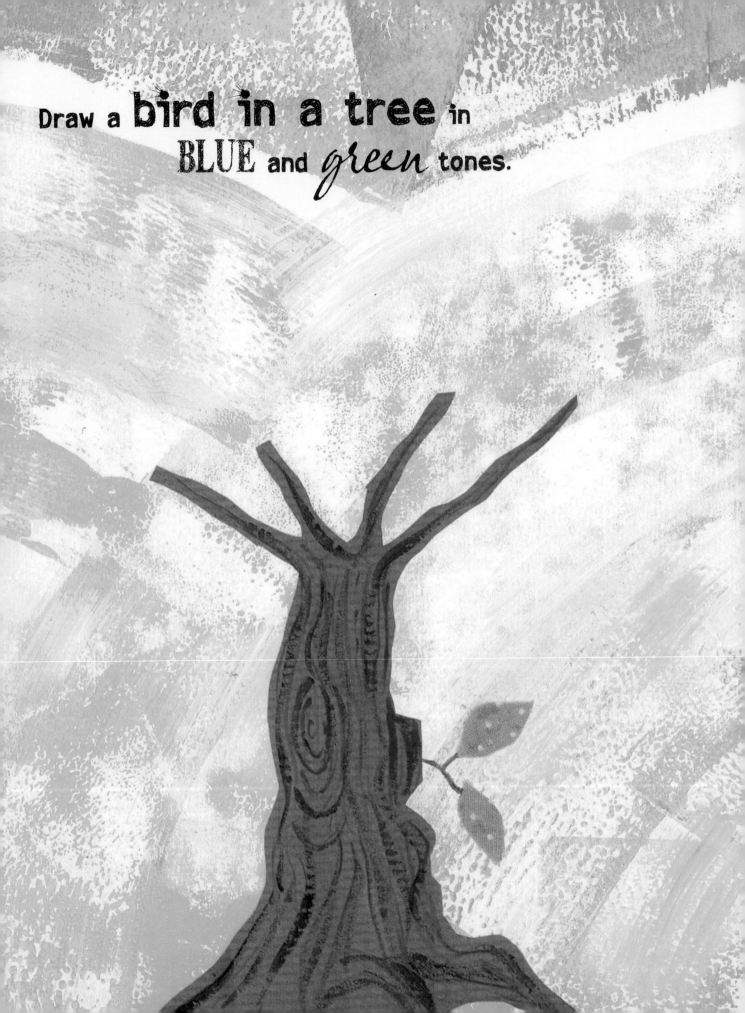

Draw a **bird in a tree** in BLUE and *green* tones.

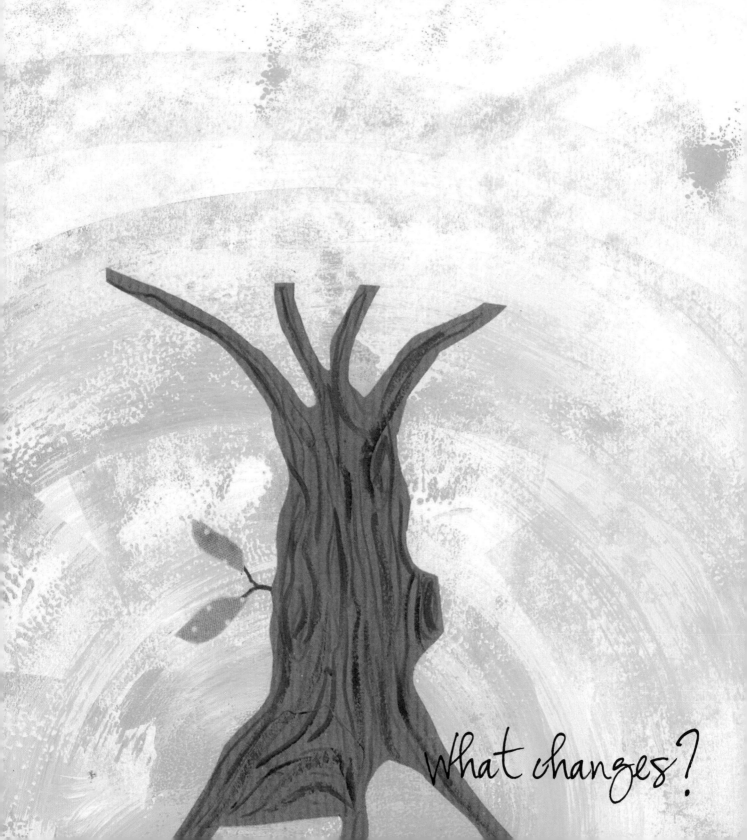

Draw a **bird in a tree** in
red and **ORANGE** tones.

What changes?

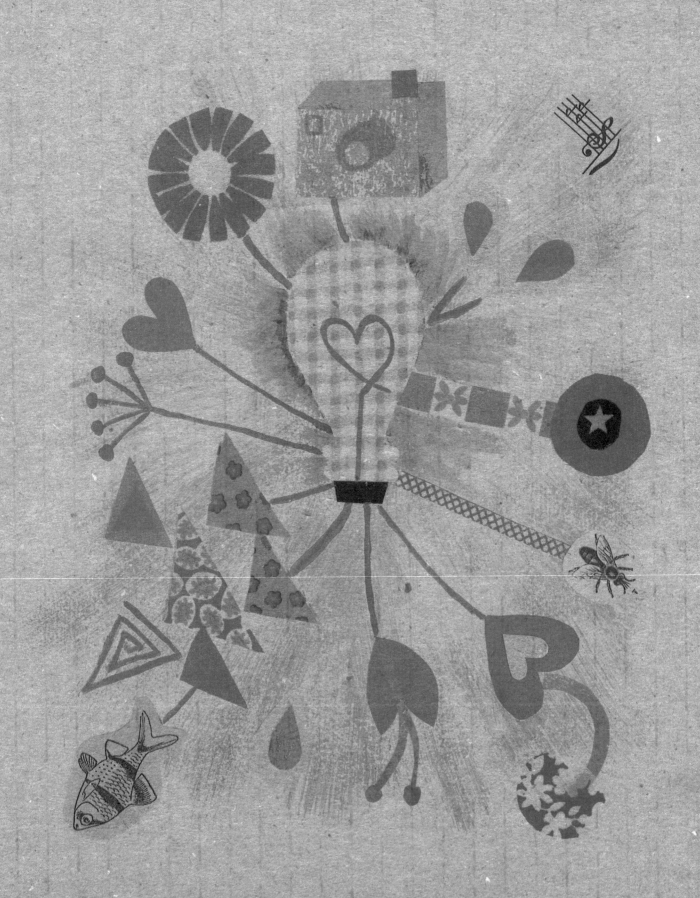

"Creativity is
INTELLIGENCE
having fun."

Albert Einstein.

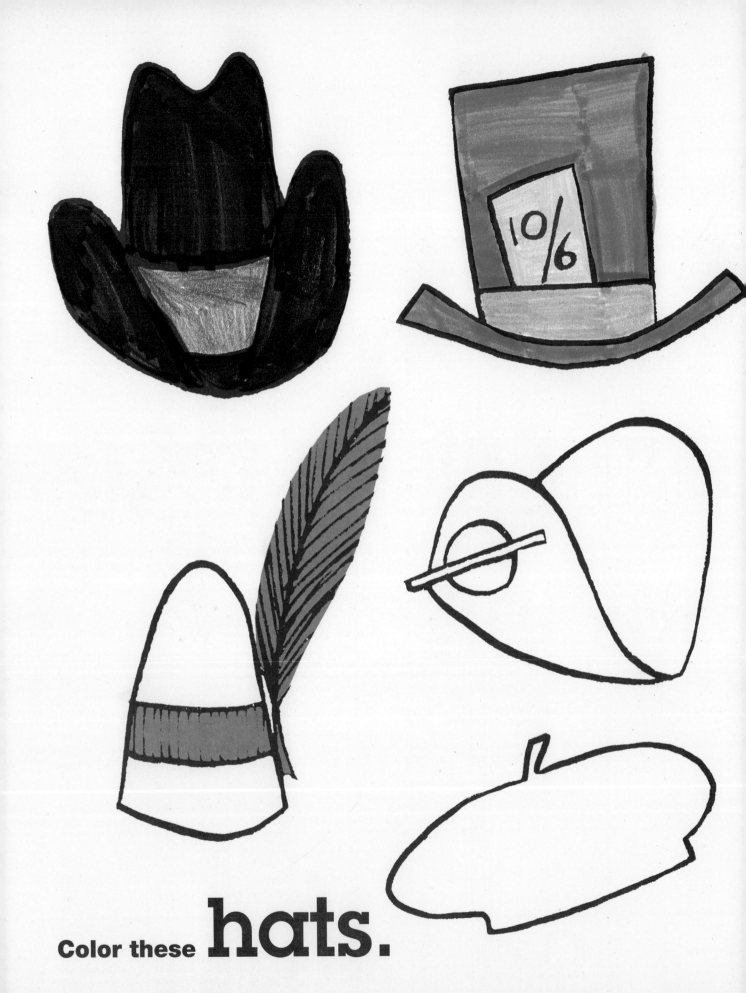

Color these hats.

Now design your own.

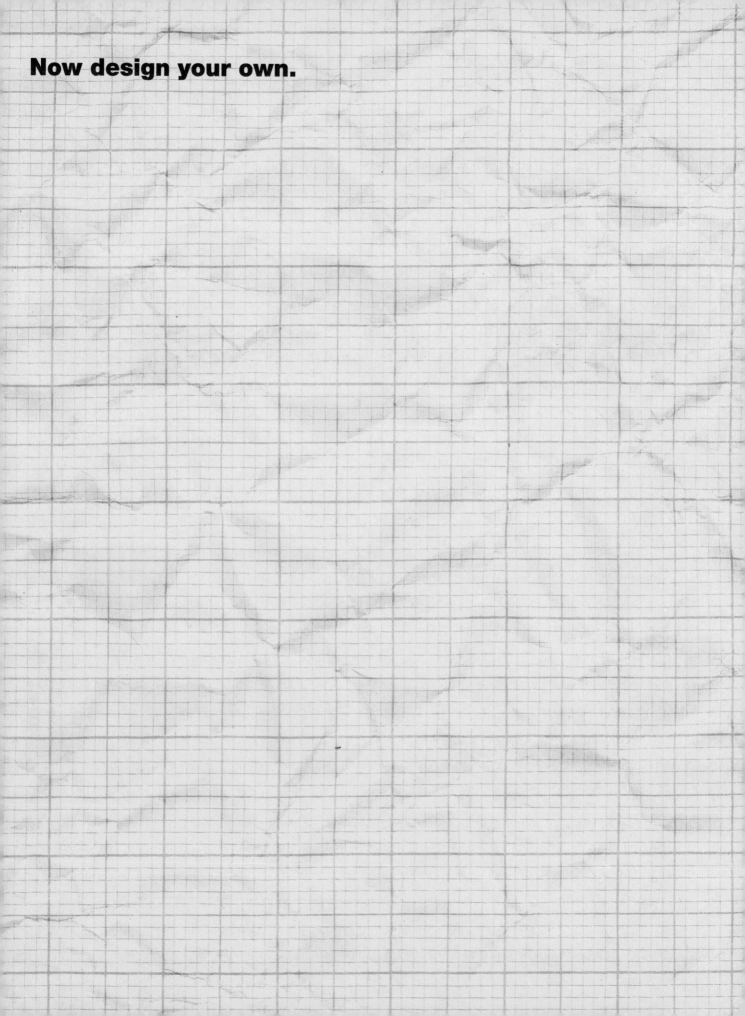

Draw the ending to your adventure story here.

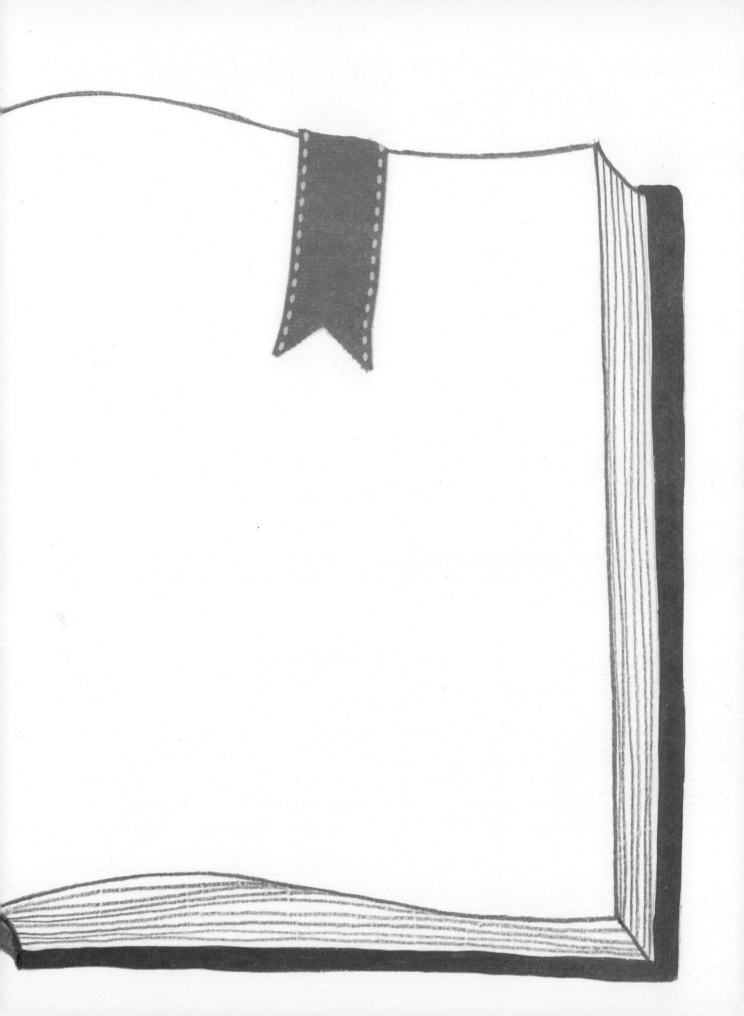

Fill this sky with things that can fly.

airplanes
butterflies
hot-air balloons

helicopters
fairies dragons
birds

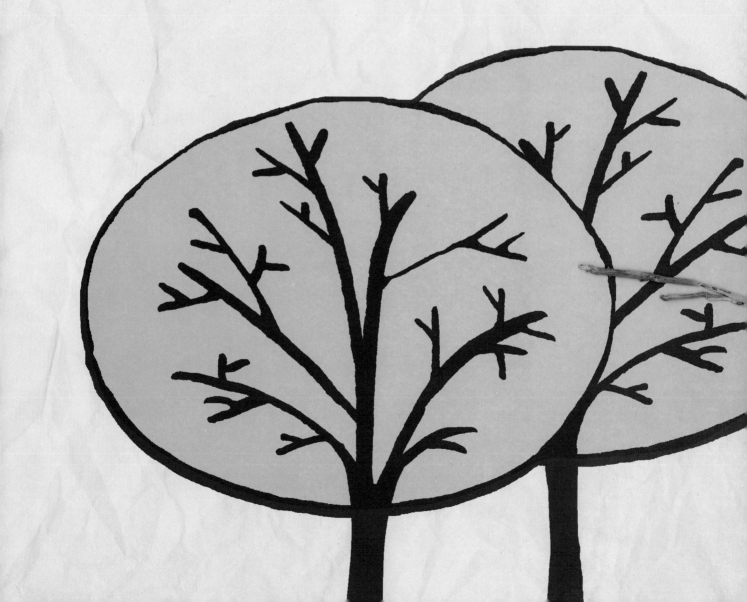

Draw your favorite TV SHOW.

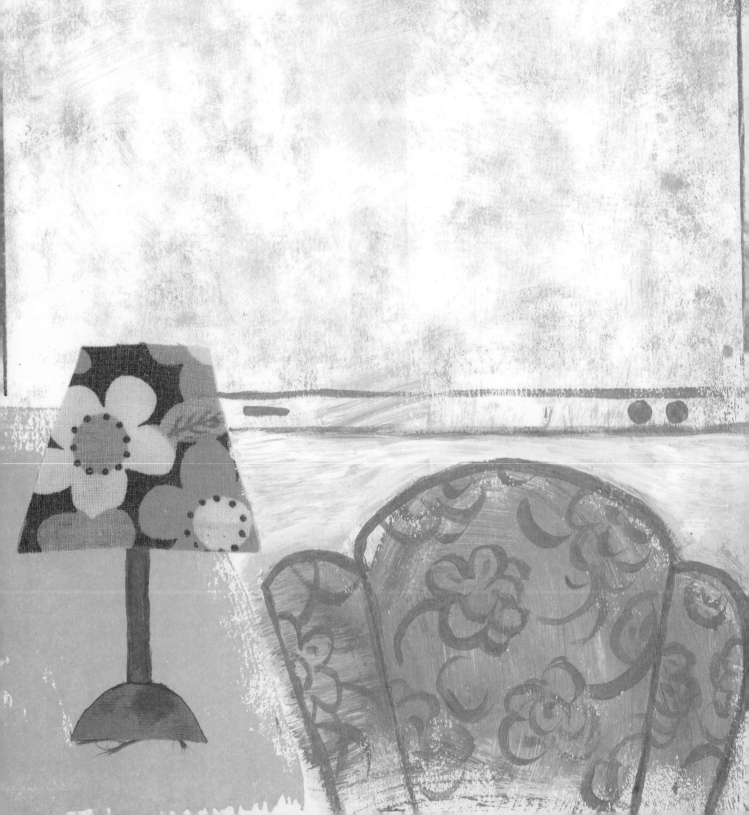

Draw your favorite MOVIE.

DON'T
THINK
JUST
DRAW.

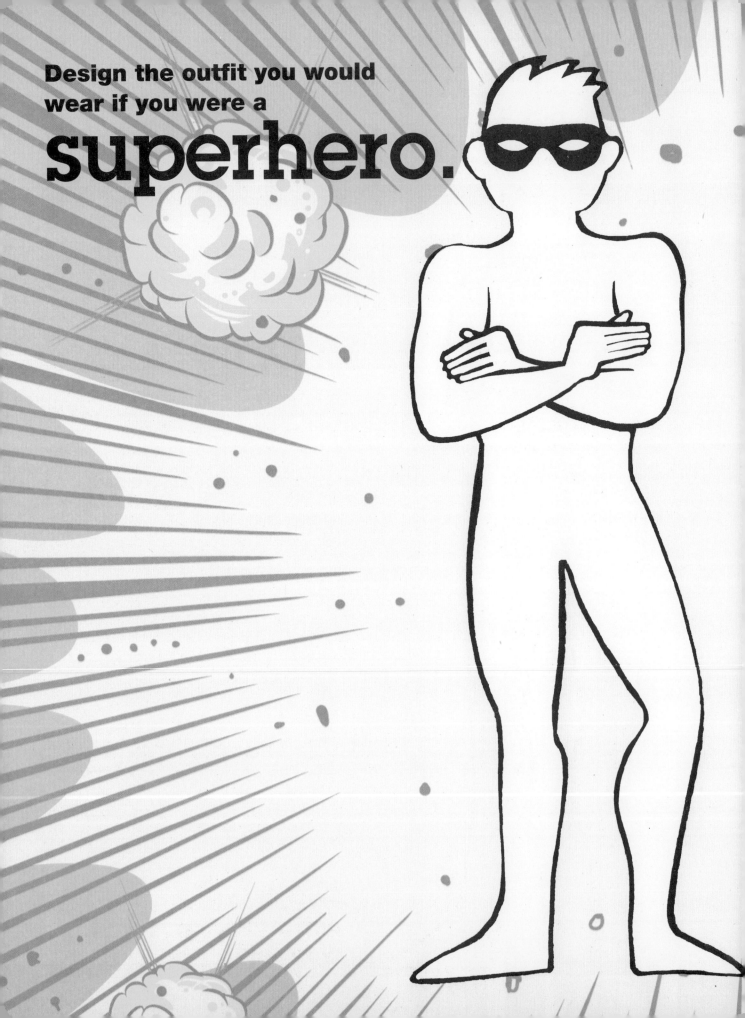

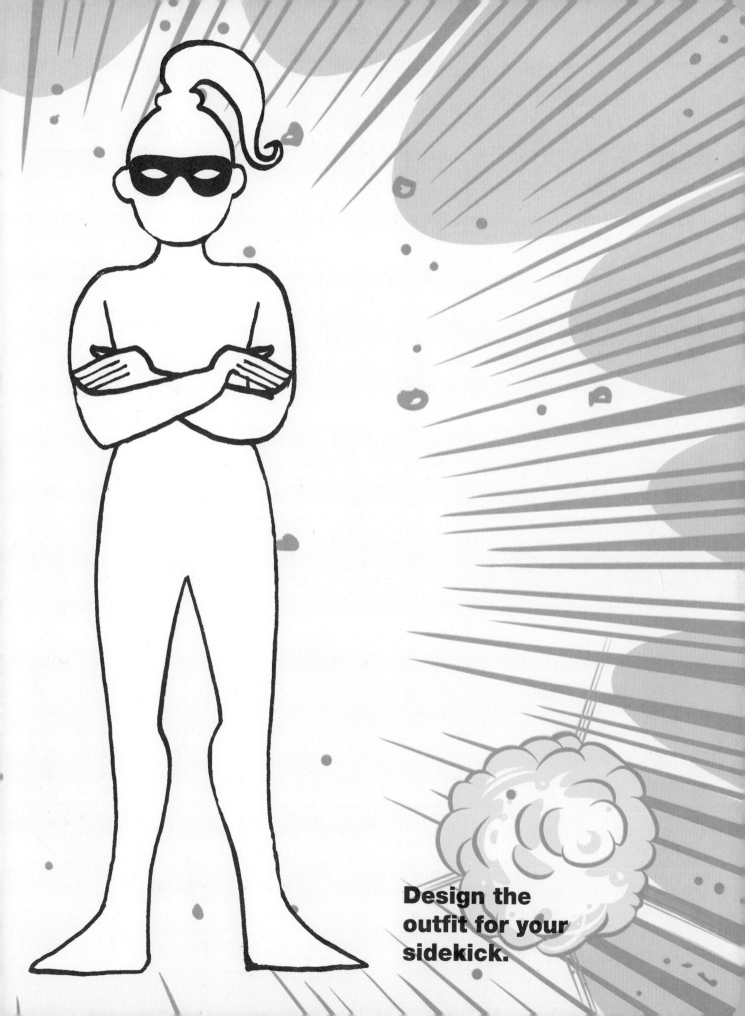

Design the outfit for your sidekick.

Draw a *portrait* of yourself from the back.

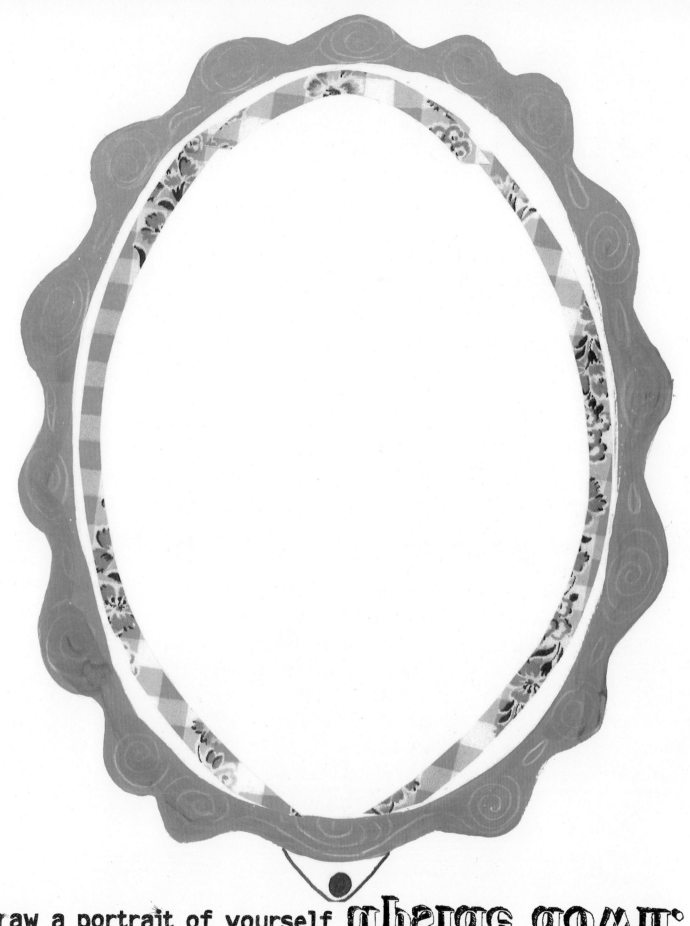

Draw a portrait of yourself upside down.

Fill this row of jars with
different size, color, and style
buttons.

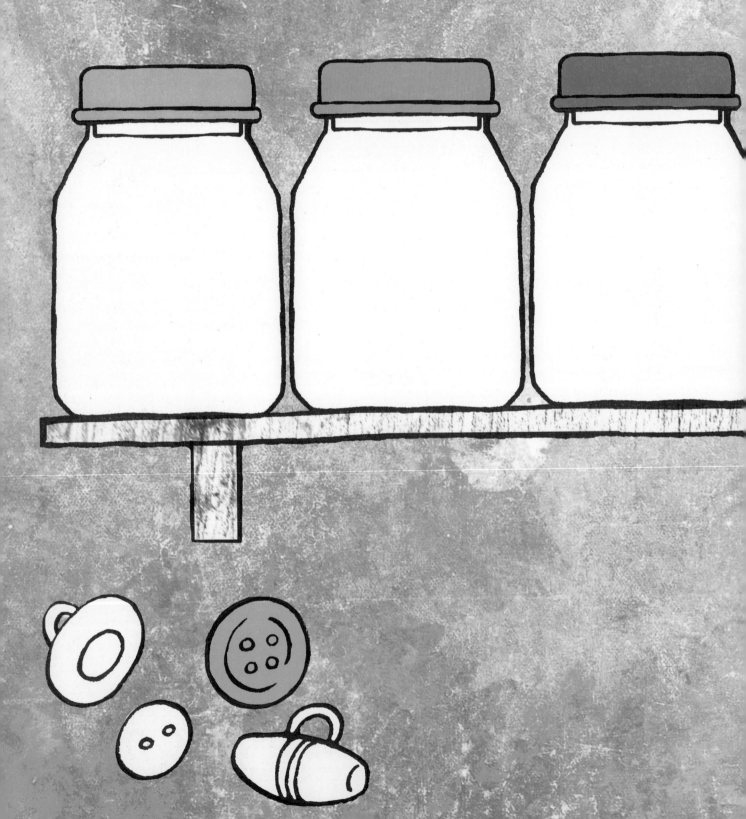

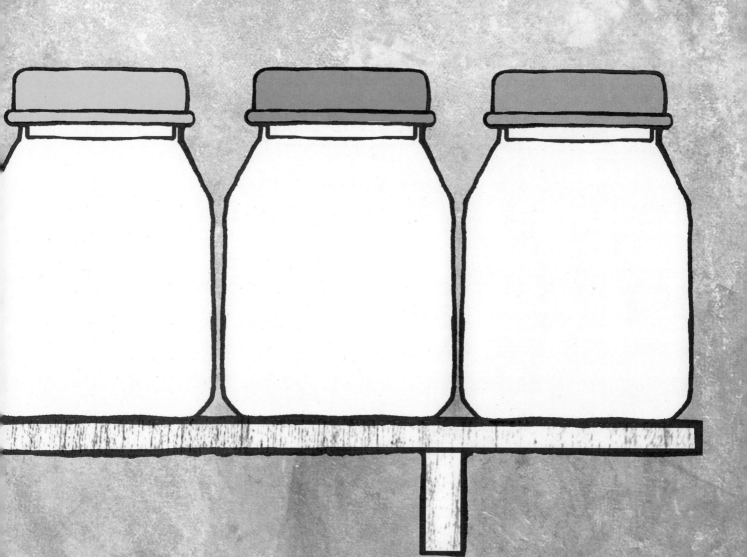

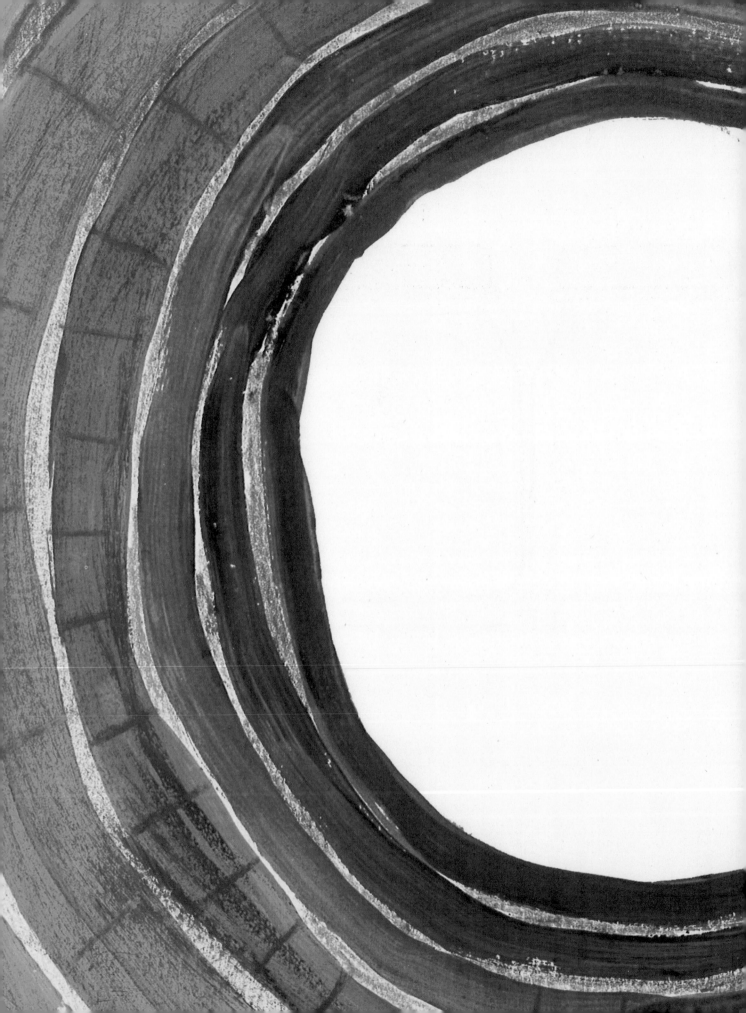

Draw what is at the **BOTTOM** of this well.

Using this graph paper create a

mosaic.

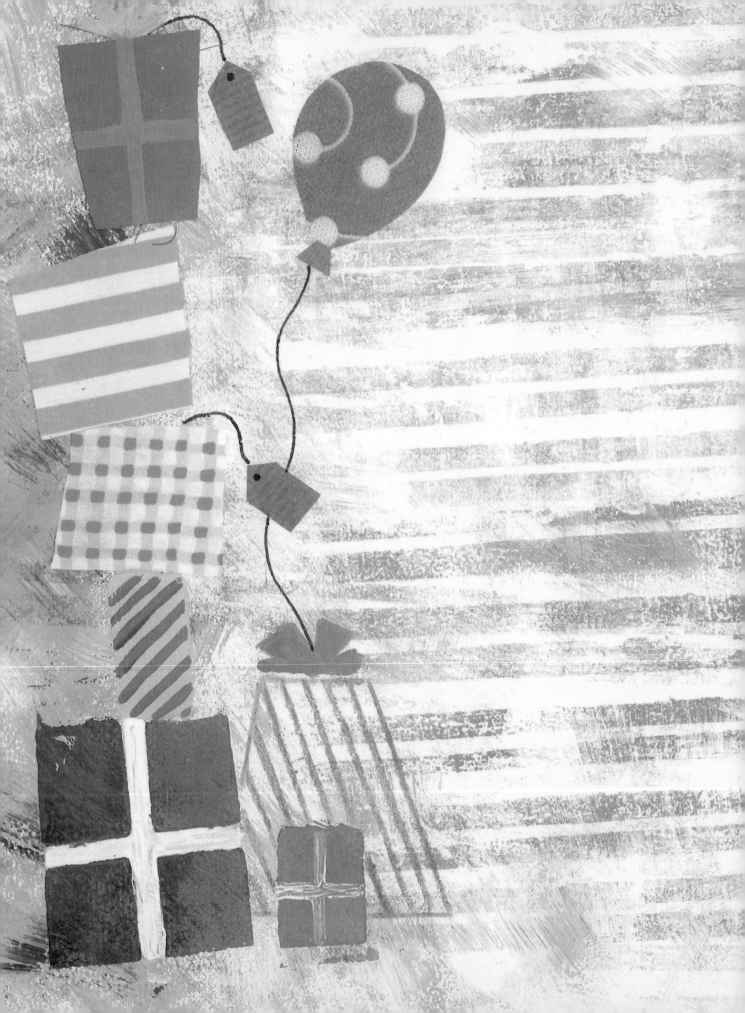

Draw something **you're looking forward to.**

Create a colorful
pattern.

**For each different color
you use try not taking your
pen from the page.**

Light a campfire.

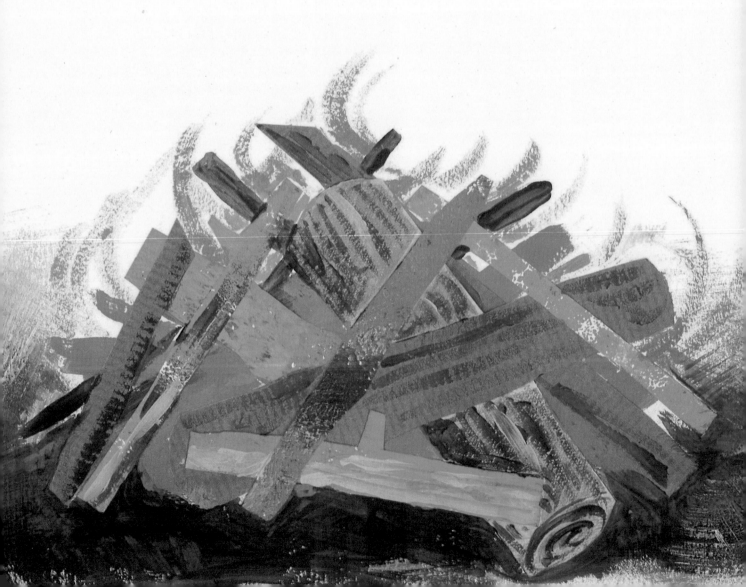

Draw the **SMOKE** billowing onto this page.

Turn this boat into a
pirate ship.

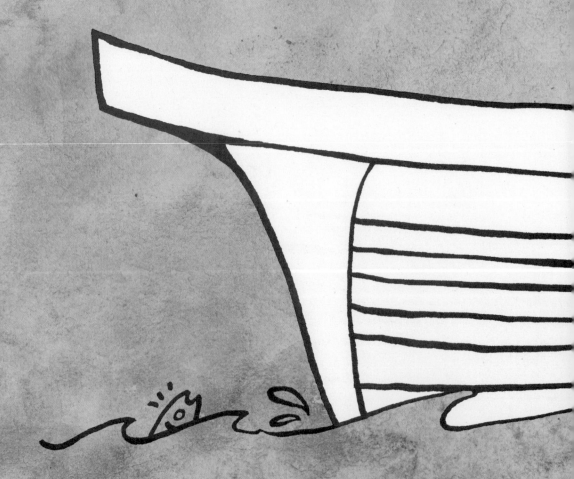

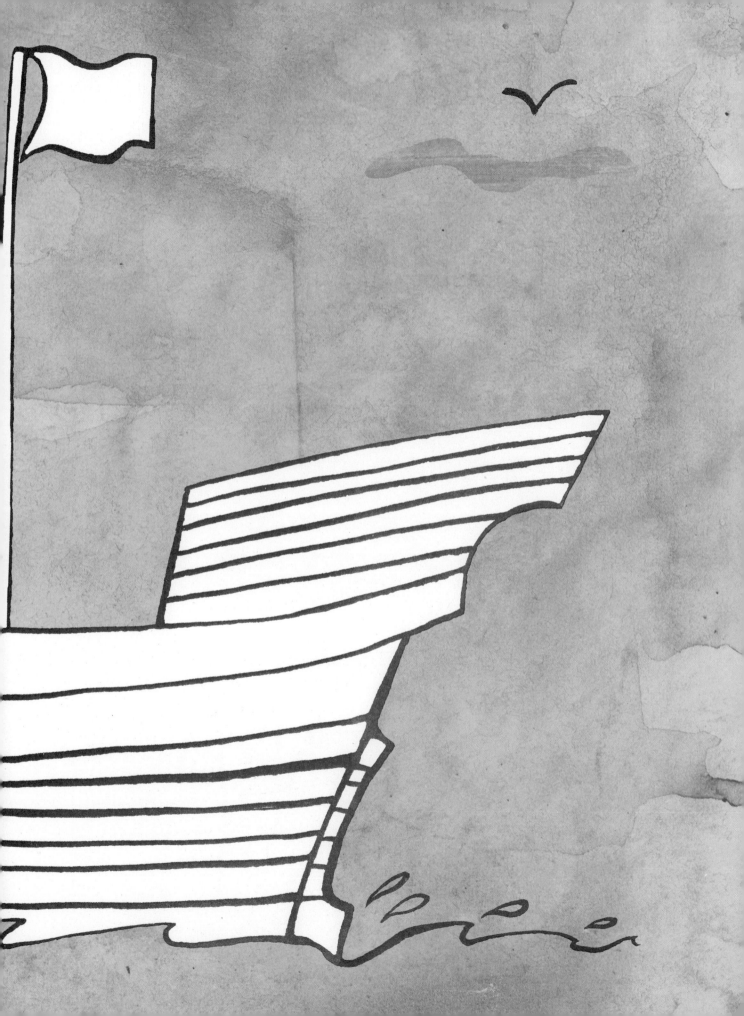

Look around and pick
out everything that is
RED.

Draw everything you see in that **color** in one picture.

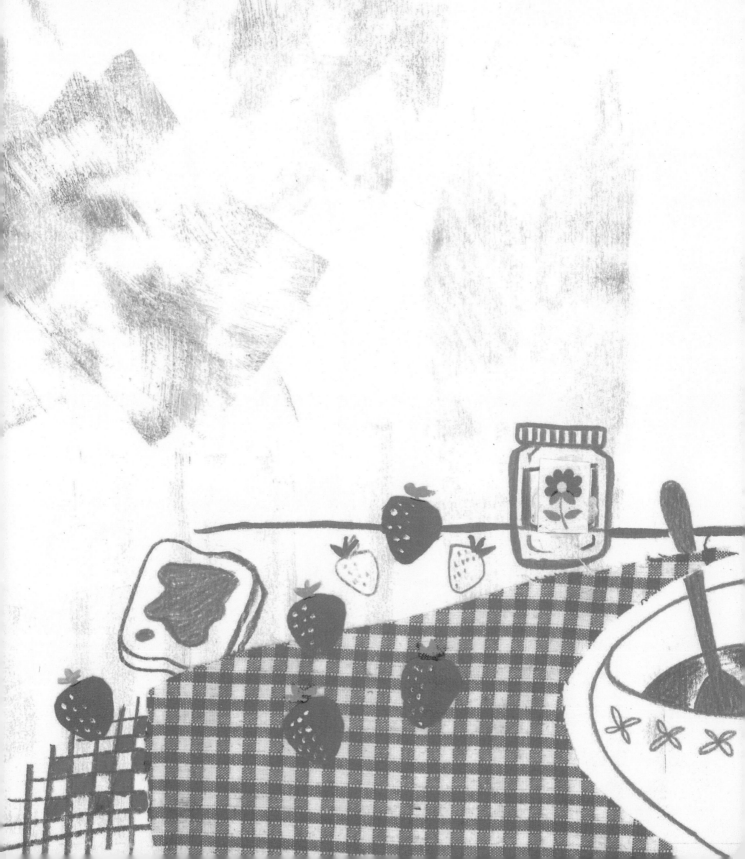

Frost this cake.

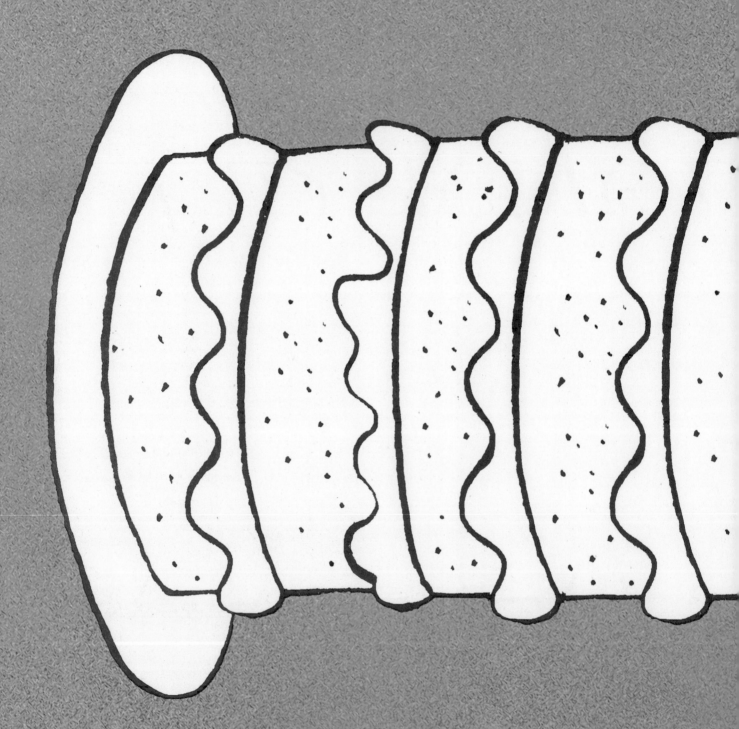

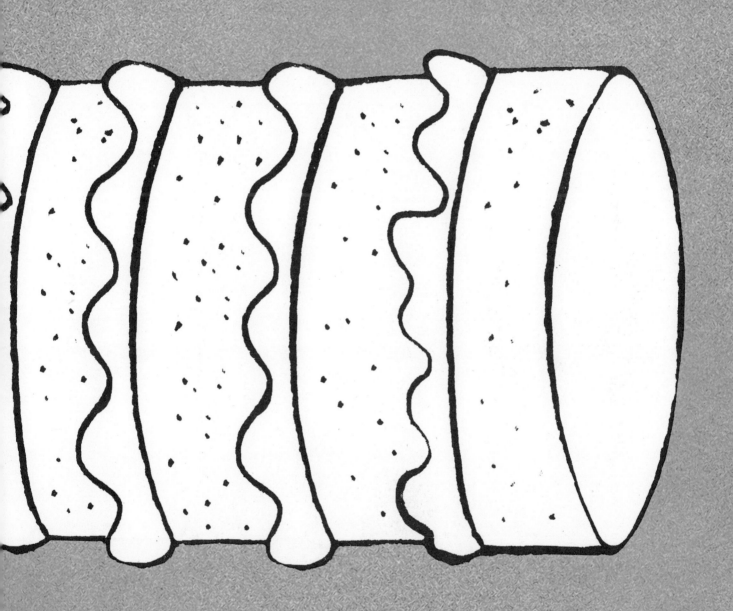

Draw something
beginning with
the letter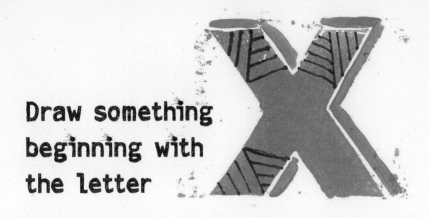

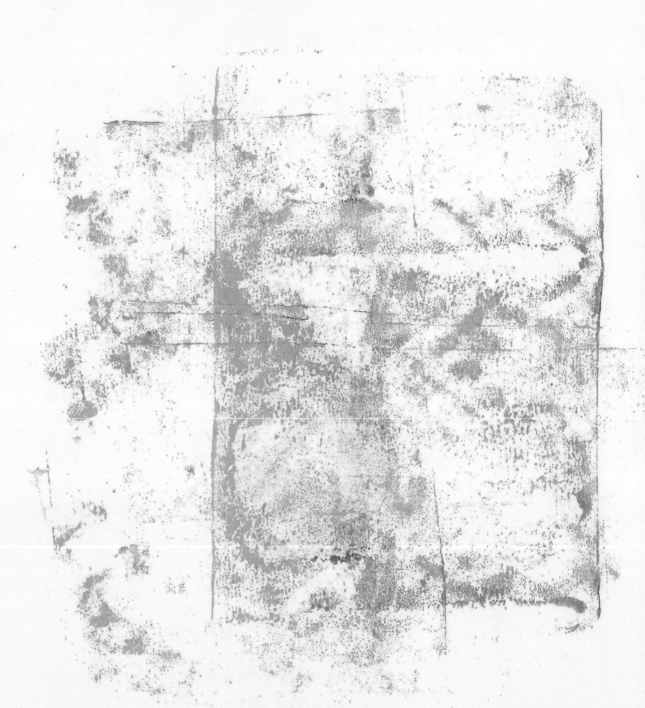

Sword Fish

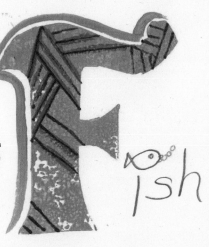

Draw something beginning with the letter Fish

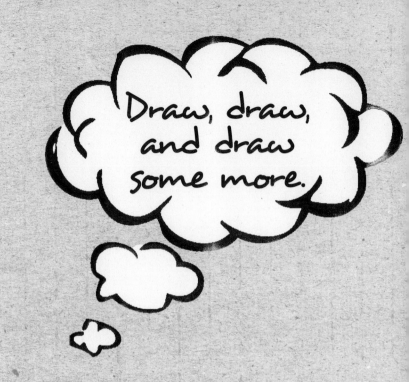

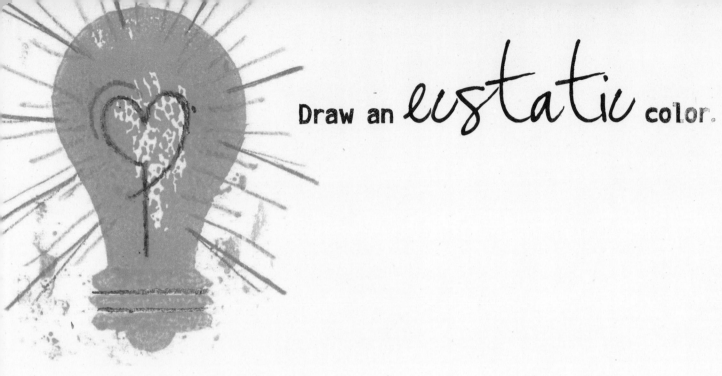

Draw an *ecstatic* color.

Draw a SAD color.

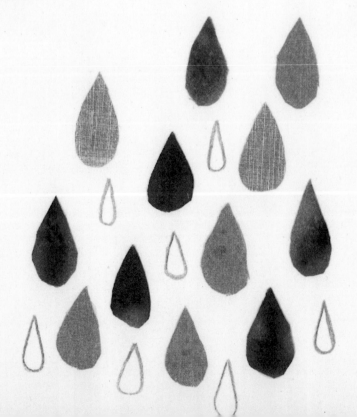

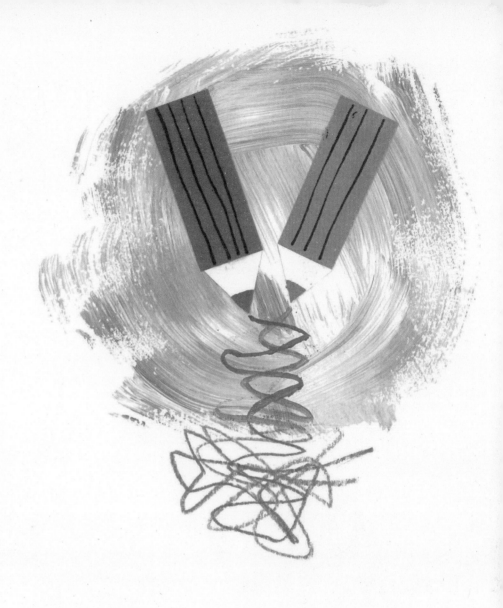

Draw PINK and RED in a fight.

Turn these shapes into monsters.

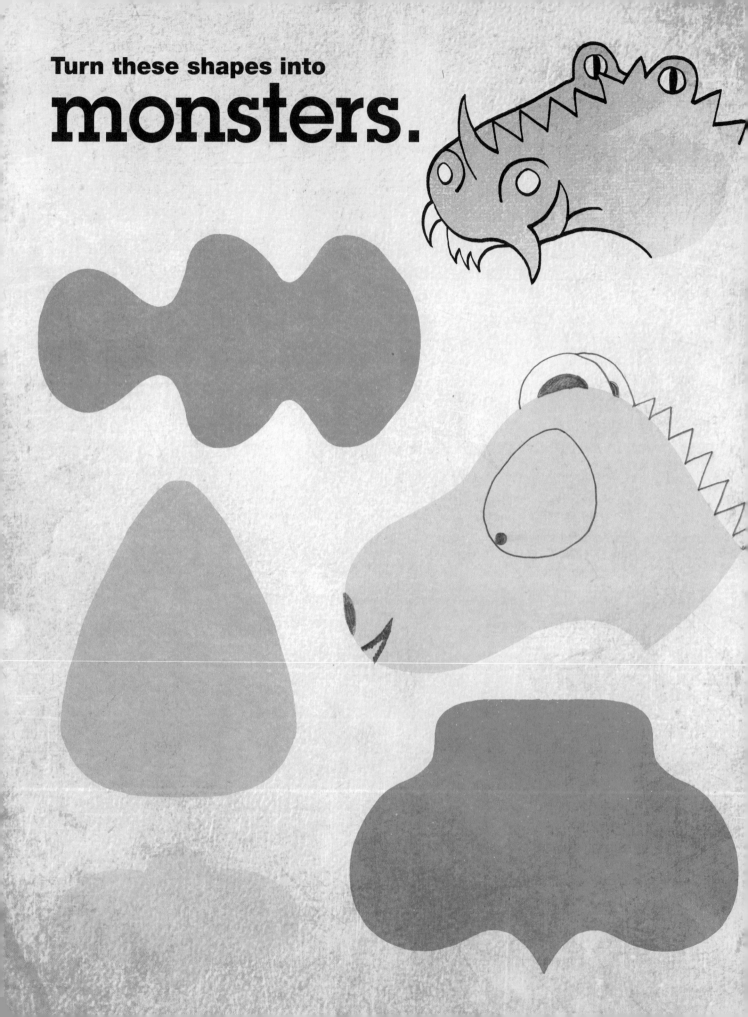

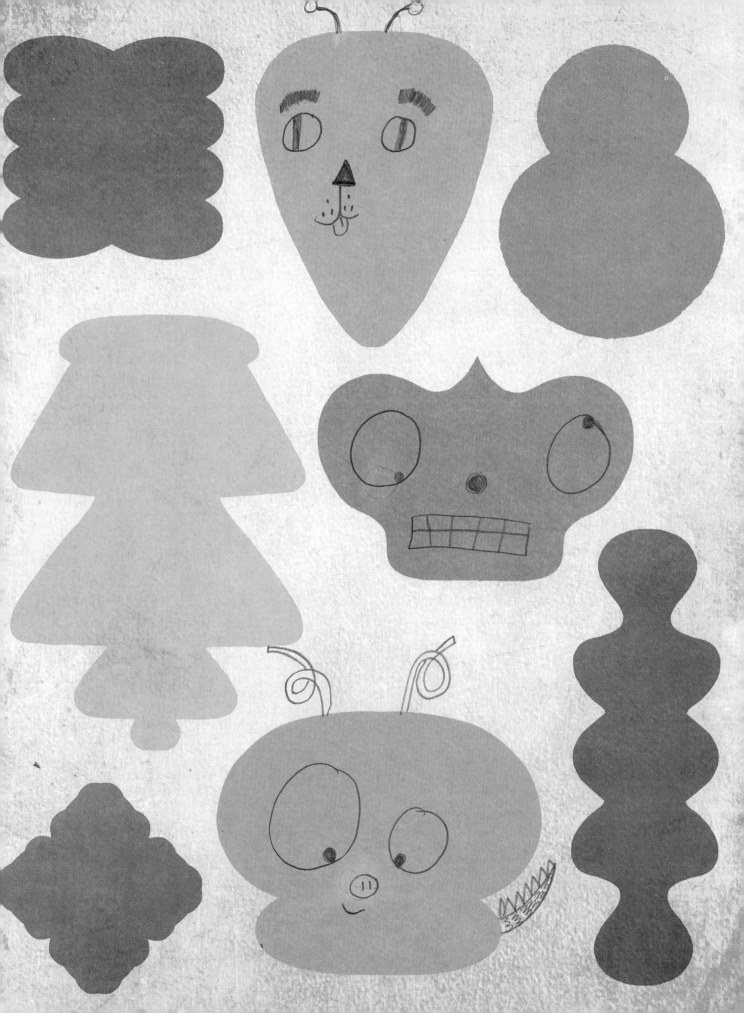

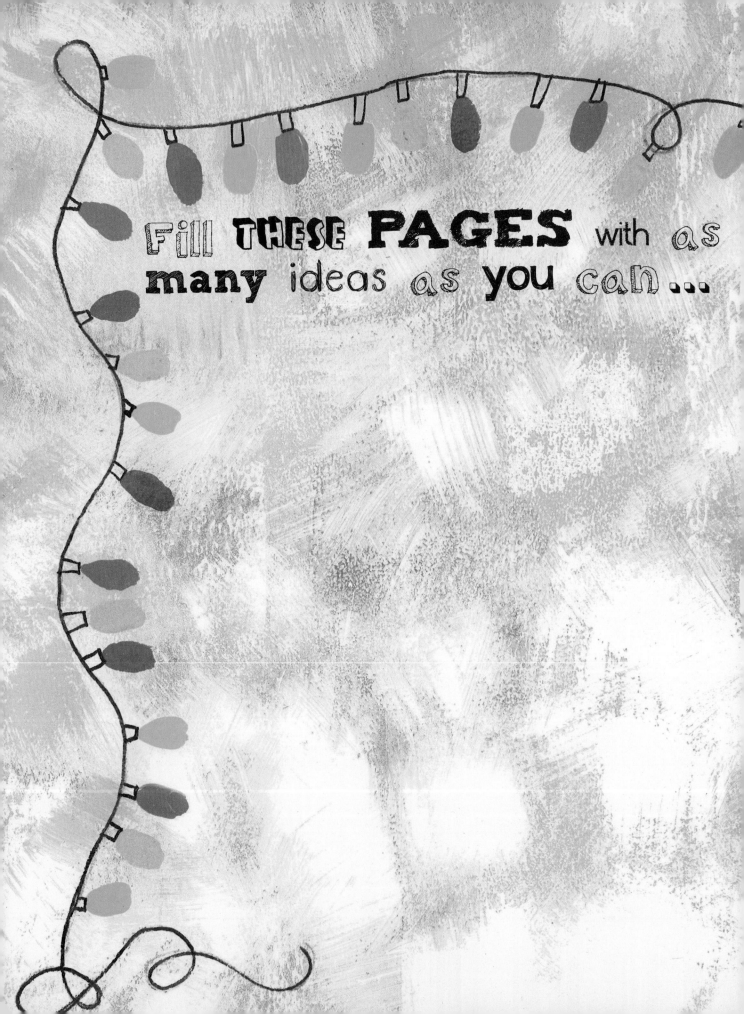

Fill THESE PAGES with as many ideas as you can ...

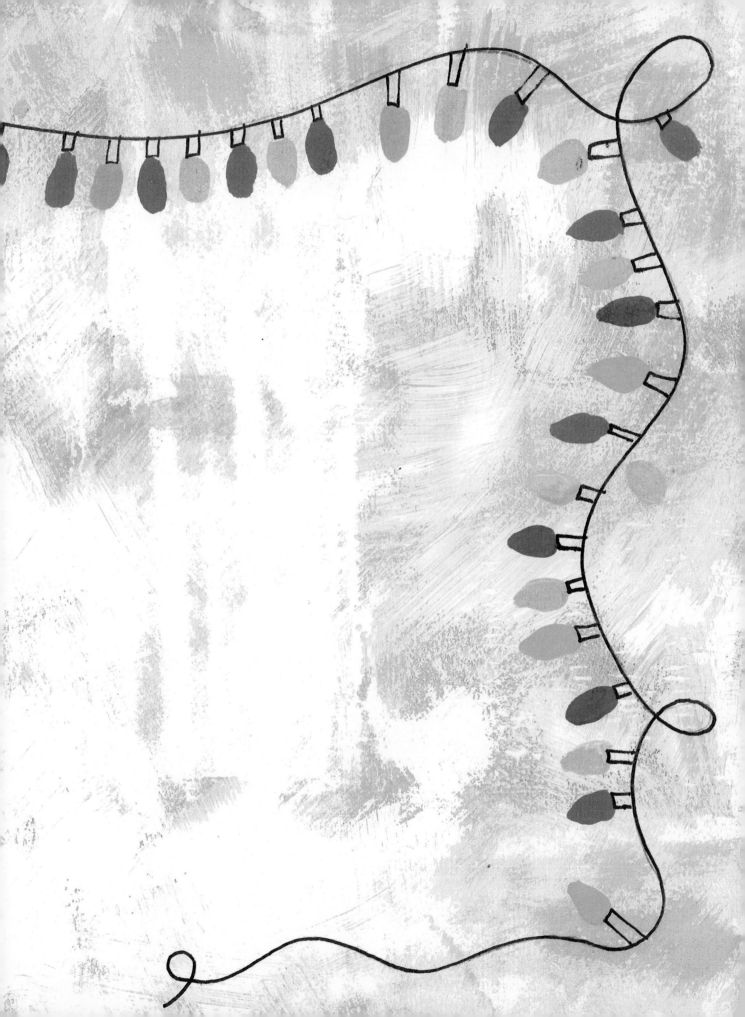

Fill these pages with
flying pigs.

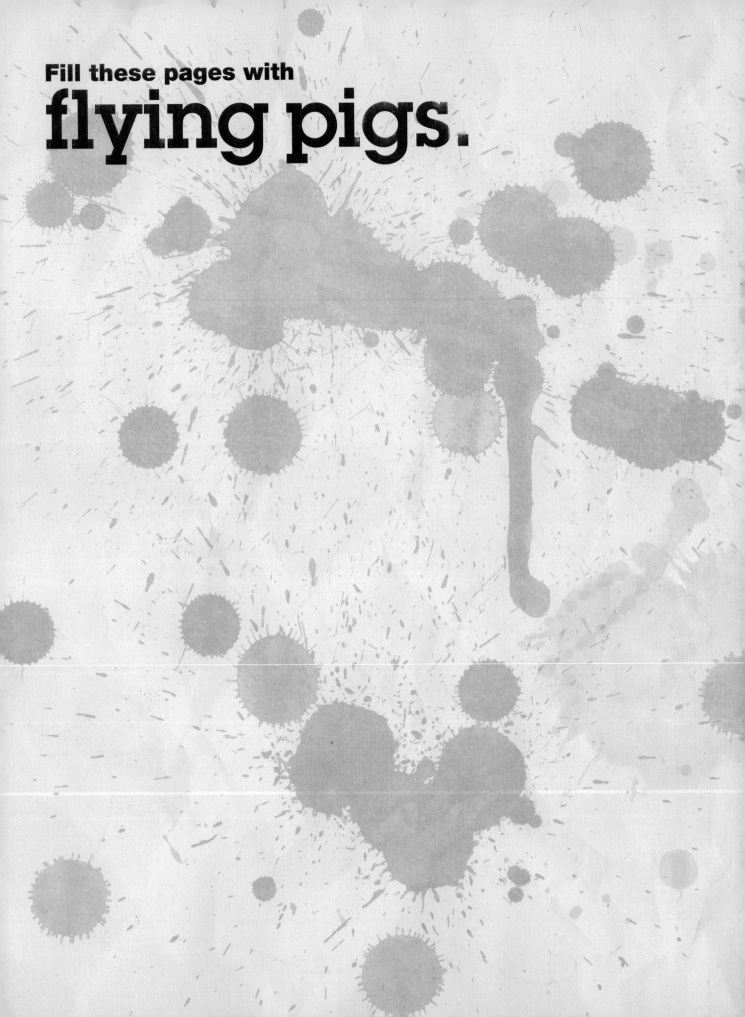

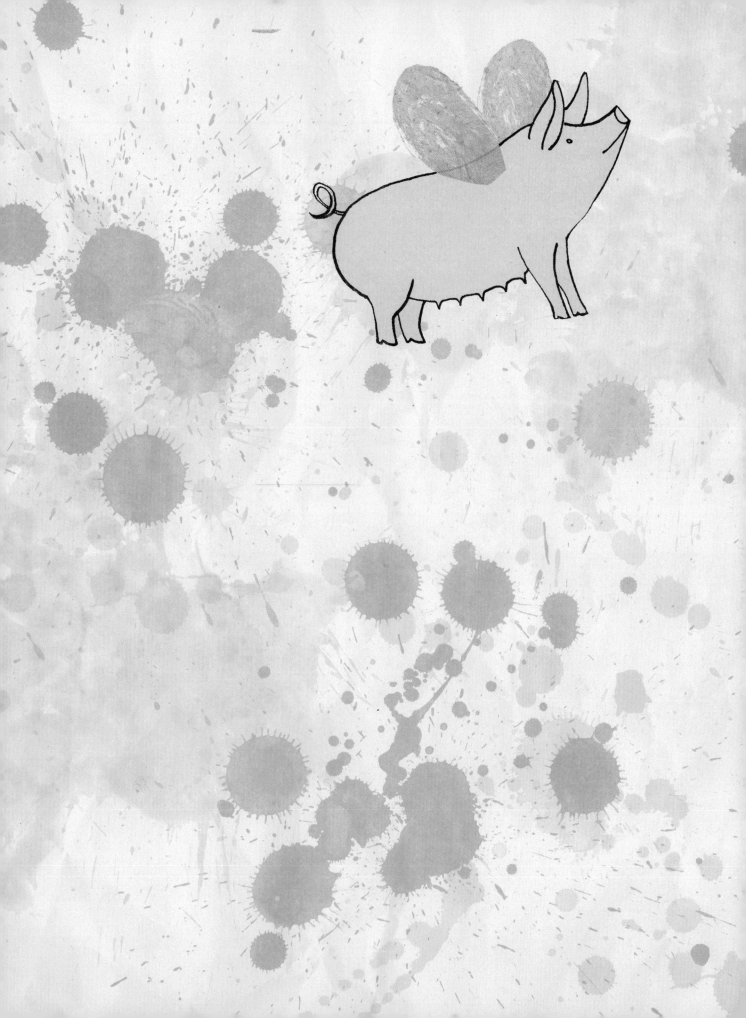

"Insp exists, but find you

iration
it has to
working."

Pablo Picasso.

Draw a
mermaid
on this rock.

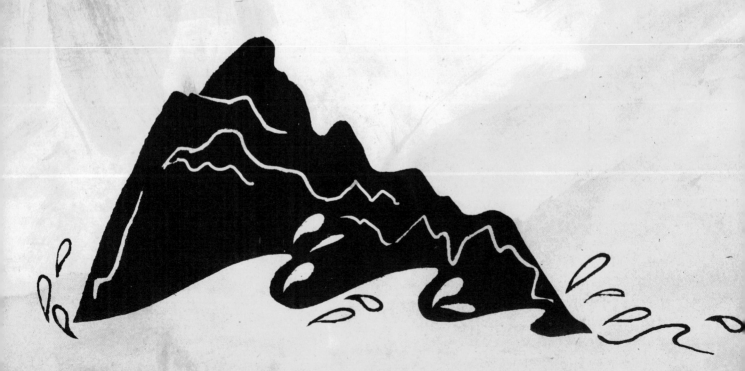